Transforming Modernity:
Popular Culture in Mexico

D0793101

 Translations from Latin America Series

Institute of Latin American Studies
University of Texas at Austin

Transforming Modernity: Popular Culture in Mexico

By Néstor García Canclini
Translated by Lidia Lozano

University of Texas Press, Austin

First Edition, 1993

Requests for permission to reproduce material from this work should be sent to Permissions, University of Texas Press, P.O. Box 7819, Austin, Texas 78713-7819

⊖ The paper used in this publication meets the minimum requirements of American National Standard for Information Sciences—Permanence of Paper for Printed Library Materials, ANSI Z39.48–1984.

All photos courtesy of Lourdes Grobet.

Library of Congress Cataloging-in-Publication Data

García Canclini, Néstor.
    [Culturas populares en el capitalismo. English]
    Transforming modernity : popular culture in Mexico / by Néstor
García Canclini ; translated by Lidia Lozano.
        p.   cm. — (Translations from Latin America series)
    Includes bibliographical references and index.
    ISBN 0-292-72758-5. — ISBN 0-292-72759-3 (pbk.)
    1. Artisans—Mexico. 2. Folk art—Mexico. 3. Cottage industries—
Mexico. 4. Mexico—Popular culture. I. Title. II. Series.
HD2346.M4G3713 1993
338.6'425'0972—dc20   92-47426
                                                CIP

Contents

Photo section, pages 48–54

Preface

What is popular culture: spontaneous creation by the people, their collective memory turned into a commodity, or the exotic representation of a state of backwardness that industry reduces to the condition of a curiosity for the sake of tourists?

The romantic solution is: to isolate creativity and manual production, the beauty and wisdom of the people, to picture sentimentally natural communities untouched by capitalist development, as if popular cultures were not also the product of the assimilation of dominant ideologies and the contradictions of oppressed classes.

The market strategy is: to recognize popular creations but not the people who make them, to rate them only in terms of profitability, and to regard crafts, *fiestas*, and "traditional" beliefs as remnants of precapitalist forms of production. The popular is another name for the primitive: an obstacle to be removed or a new category of commodities to help increase sales to consumers unhappy with mass production.

What tourists see are: ornaments for sale to decorate their apartments; "savage" ceremonies, testimonies to the superiority of their own society; and symbols of assorted and remote travels, and therefore of their own purchasing power. Culture is like nature: a show. Sunny beaches and Indian dances are regarded alike. The past blends with the present, people or stones—it is all the same: a Day of the Dead ceremony and a Mayan pyramid are sets in which to be photographed.

This book seeks to understand the various manifestations of popular culture in their totality: why it spreads to what people make, what is sold in markets and boutiques, and the shows into which the mass media turn our daily lives. Instead of holding onto an illusory authenticity, as is the case with romantic escapism, I will attempt to explain why Indians make their crafts and *fiestas* increasingly for others, to be bought and looked at. In order to avoid limiting my argument to the—central—issue of the commercialization of culture, I will explore the economic and symbolic aspects of popular goods, what is sold and what is sought after.

I will also seek to establish how the meaning of what people make in a workshop complements what another sector of the population uses in its urban household or watches on television: since all settings of popular culture are part of the capitalist system, we must find a way to understand them in their totality.

To redefine what constitutes popular culture today, we need a research strategy that enables us to include the realms of production, circulation, and consumption. To understand, for example, why handmade articles have not just survived but in fact increased in industrial societies, we must ask ourselves why the social system boosts their production. We have to give up, then, both a notion that reduces crafts to a collection of objects and popular culture to a set of traditions, as well as the folkloric idealism that believes it is possible to explain popular creations as the autonomous "expression" of a people's genius. The most fruitful approach is one that regards culture as a tool helpful for understanding, reproducing, and transforming the social system, and for making and constructing the hegemony of individual classes. From this viewpoint, we will consider the cultures of popular classes as the product of unequal appropriation of cultural capital, their own reflections about their living conditions, and conflict-ridden interaction with hegemonic sectors.

This theoretical and methodological approach, which will be developed in the first two chapters, centers around the following hypotheses:

1. Capitalist modernization, particularly in the case of a dependent capitalism with strong Indian roots, does not always destroy traditional cultures as it moves forward; it can also appropriate them, restructure them, reorganize the meaning and function of their objects, beliefs, and practices. Its favorite devices, as we shall see in chapter 3, are restructuring rural and urban production and consumption and promoting tourism and state policies for ideological refunctionalization.

2. In order to integrate the popular classes into the process of capitalist development, the dominant classes destructure ethnic, class, and national cultures through a series of different processes—all of them, though, subject to a common logic—and reorganize them into a unified system of symbolic production. To achieve this, they separate the economic basis from cultural representations and break the unity between production, circulation, and consumption and between individuals and the community. At a second stage, or simultaneously, they put the pieces back together again and subordinate them to a globalization of culture that corresponds to the nationalization of capital. We will examine this process through one of its principal mechanisms: the reduction of the ethnic to the typical (chap. 4).

However, since we will also be looking at the response to domination by traditional communities and mestizo villages, their ways of adapting to it, resisting, or finding a space to survive, the final objective of this book will be to put forward an interpretation of intercultural conflicts under capitalist modernization.

This interpretation began to take shape in a study of changes in popular crafts and *fiestas* carried out between 1977 and 1980 in central Mexico, among villages in the Tarascan area of the state of Michoacán. I explored two regions with similar ethnic origin, but different economic and cultural development: (1) the area surrounding Lake Pátzcuaro, which is closely integrated into the process of capitalist economic development, tourism, communications, and action of official organizations; and (2) Patamban and Ocumicho, small pottery and farming villages in the *sierra*, based on the domestic unit of production and accessible only by dirt road. They still speak partly Tarascan and hold *fiestas* and fairs that only recently have begun to see tourists and manufactured goods.

To carry out a comparative study of the influence of external agents and the evolution of these two types of villages, I have considered changes I observed through the years during visits, as well as the earlier structure, crafts, and *fiestas* of each village, as related in reports by Mexican or American anthropologists since the forties.[1] This study differs from previous ones in that I was interested not only in looking at life within the villages but also in following artisans and their goods to *fiestas* and markets—in Pátzcuaro, Morelia, and the Federal District—to learn about their interaction with people and institutions outside their place of origin and to establish how urban consumption lends a new meaning to the material and symbolic production of traditional cultures.

Earlier lengthy accounts of the Tarascan region provided a background to my own fieldwork and saved me from having to include detailed ethnographic descriptions in some chapters. Since both general and detailed accounts are available, I have concentrated on providing empirical data on recent intercultural processes as yet unexplored and on developing the analytical framework necessary to understand them: this has guided the selection of descriptions and data, though I have also included some historical and other basic information to help readers unfamiliar with Michoacán acquaint themselves with the region. Anyone wishing to obtain a more detailed overview of the area will find it in the works cited in note 1 above, particularly in the books by Carrasco, Dinerman, Novelo, and Van Zantwijk.

While the clash beween the old culture and the contemporary redefinition of functions structures the entire book, the issue is given particular attention in chapters 5 and 6. In chapter 5, we follow the process of decontextualizaton and redefinition of functions undergone by crafts in different social spaces and classes: Indian households, peasant markets and fairs, shops and boutiques, museums, and urban households. In chapter 6, we focus on the role of nondurable crafts in Indian *fiestas*, on what turns such celebrations into shows, collective participation into planned consumption, and the farming–religious ritual order into the commercial organization of tourists' leisure.

The approach used here to these subjects and methodology place this book somewhere between the realms of anthropology and sociology. However, the reader will also find political and philosophical reflections on culture. As we explore the changing identity of popular cultures, we critically examine the reasons behind, and the dilemmas faced by, those institutions that promote them, as well as the direction that cultural policies—both rural and urban—should follow during a process of social change.

At the same time, research on ephemeral and changeable elements in cultural processes leads us to reflect on the fragile and unstable aspects of culture, not just traditional ones under the impact of capitalist modernization, but all representations with which individuals attempt to account for their lives. Given that the symbolic cannot be reduced to observable patterns of behavior and their immediate practical objectives, I believe that the study of social conditions of production must include the utopian or searching aspects of culture. The anthropological interpretation of the *fiesta* of the dead, for example, offers an opportunity to understand what individuals try to do, through the *fiesta*, that they cannot do with death. The study of these ceremonies and offerings will help us to see culture not only as a manifestation of how people live under capitalism, but also of how they die and how they remember; it will enable us to see how the art of the poor reworks the material and concrete conditions of society, as well as what it imagines beyond them.

In considering these uncertainties concerning the fate of popular cultures in class conflict that tends to erode them, one must question the future and value of all culture, representations, systems of thought, and beliefs through which we seek to explain and justify ourselves. The analysis of conditionings that act upon culture and of culture as an instrument for the reproduction of objective social relations prevails throughout the book. However, we do not go so far as to tell which are the elements, present in all symbolic production, that involve the invention of new realities, games about reality, and openings, or windows, to what is not or to what we cannot become. How can we understand those refutations of reality that we keep on constructing in the palaces of the world of dreams, in utopian and literary archetypes, in the profitless expenditure of a *fiesta*, in every strategy of the imaginary realm and the rhetorical tricks of desire? Why do these fictitious creations survive and expand in a world that repeatedly seeks to be subjected to the rationality of efficiency? While our capacity to transcend material needs and project ourselves toward a future that does not automatically derive from economic development cannot be regarded as the fundamental and distinctive feature of humankind, as idealism might argue, it does nonetheless merit a place in an interpretation of culture. We also want to discuss these topics from a sociohistorical approach, because we recognize the social—and even political—significance of reconceptualizing those elements that idealism, by isolating them under the name of genius, left unexplained, and mechanistic materialism, by reducing them to their conditionings, left without any specificity of their own.

Acknowledgments

Research for this book, carried out between 1977 and 1980, was supported and financed by the Escuela Nacional de Antropología e Historia de México. The following students assisted at different stages: Tania Carrasco, Ana María Cofiño, Susana Ferrucci, Gracia Imberton, Mónica Maldonado, Elia Nora Moretti Sánchez, Leticia Rivermar Pérez, María Rocío Súarez Reyes, Javier Tellez, Sonia Toledo Tello, and Patricia Vara Orozco.

I want to convey my thanks to those who helped me reflect on the topics dealt with in this book and suggested changes to the manuscript: Marta Dujovne, Clarisa Hardy, María Eugenia Módena, Victoria Novelo, Mercedes Olivera, Daniel Prieto, and Mariángela Rodríguez.

It would take several pages to acknowledge all the artisans, dancers, officials, traders, and even tourists who provided me with information. I would like to mention some of those artisans who received me generously and even invited me to stay in their homes, but it would be unfair to pick just a few names. Besides, as chapter 4 will show when we discuss the indifference of artisans toward those who ask them to sign their work, I know that, instead of individual acknowledgment, they hope to see their ideas spread and their work understood and protected.

Transforming Modernity:
Popular Culture in Mexico

1. From the Primitive to the Popular: Theories about Inequality between Cultures

It is the same with culture, the traditional object of anthropology, as with objects from communities studied by it: the most common elements, water or the sun, are called by different names as we cross from one side of the mountain to the other. Similarly, cultural facts, present in every society, receive different names, depending on which discipline is involved. A student becoming acquainted with this field of knowledge for the first time discovers that the natives of one particular science call them symbolic systems, while others call them signs, or ideology, or communication, or the imaginary.

Why do we choose to talk of culture? Why classify this particular form of culture that others call subordinate, oppressed, and so on, as popular culture? While in all areas of research theory must develop alongside empirical knowledge, this is all the more necessary within such a controversial area, such a jungle of definitions (anthropological, sociological, semiotic, and from other disciplines) that as early as 1952 amounted to three hundred, according to Kroeber's and Kluckhohn's summary.[1]

We will begin by considering the main definitions of culture offered by anthropology and the manner in which culture has been conceptualized in opposition to nature, with the hope of establishing a universally valid definition, free from ethnocentric prejudices. Then we will look at the "answer" offered by many anthropologists to the question of cultural differences—relativism—and consider it in the light of the global organization imposed on cultures by capitalism and the search for identity among liberation movements in dependent countries. The critique of the scientific and political value of anthropology's contribution will lead us to link the concept of culture to those of production, superstructure, ideology, hegemony, and social classes, as developed by Marxism. We will thus characterize culture as a particular type of production, whose objective is to understand, reproduce, and transform the social structure and to struggle for hegemony. In order to link this definition to empirical research, we will draw from some contributions to the field of sociology of culture that specify the mechanisms through which cultural capital is passed on and is internalized by individuals, thus forming habits and practices—that is to say, the structure of everyday life.

What is proposed here, then, is a change in the usual object of study. Instead of a theoretical framework to analyze *culture*, we want one that will help explain inequalities and conflicts between cultural systems. It is my belief that as the book unfolds it will become clear that this approach is the most fruitful one for the definition and study of popular cultures: just as there is no culture in general, neither can popular culture be characterized by its essence or by a set of intrinsic qualities. It must be defined in opposition to the dominant culture, as a product of inequality and conflict.

Praise for "Primitive Peoples" as Denial of History

The anthropological concept of history is the paradoxical product of Western imperialist expansion. The same confrontation between colonial and colonized countries that promoted hopes about European superiority brought about a confrontation between English, French, and American scholars and the daily life of conquered societies. As they became detached from their own culture, anthropologists began to discover alternative forms of rationality and life. They also observed that non-Western cultures had resolved perhaps in a more satisfactory manner than we the organization of the family and education and the integration of adolescents into sexual life and economic activities (e.g., the case of Margaret Mead in Polynesia).

From these discoveries, a different conception of other societies and of itself grew in the West. The dismissal of primitive peoples, similar in many ways to the devaluation of popular culture, proved to be inconsistent. The scope given to the concept of culture thereafter—that which is not nature, everything produced by the whole of humanity, regardless of the degree of complexity and development reached—represented an attempt to recognize the dignity of those excluded. All human activities, material or ideal—even those practices or beliefs previously regarded as expressions of ignorance (superstitions, human sacrifices) and social norms and simple methods of individuals living naked in the jungle, subject to the rhythms and uncertainties of nature—were considered part of culture. All cultures, however simple they might be, are structured and have coherence and meaning within themselves. Even those practices that upset us or that we reject (anthropophagy, polygamy) are logical within the society that approves of them and are functional to its existence.

Perhaps Lévi-Strauss is one of the anthropologists who argued most cohesively the logical and structured character of archaic cultures and tore down most painstakingly the Western claim to represent the culmination of history and to have advanced furthest in the appropriation and use of nature, in rationality and scientific thought. His research on racism for UNESCO[2] offers the case of America to refute the evolutionary notion of human history as a single linear and progressive movement, with European culture at its apex and others representing earlier stages of the same process. Before the Spanish Conquest, the inhabitants of the New World had reached an impressive level of cultural development, independently of Europe: they had domesticated animals and plants, obtained unique cures and beverages, and developed industries such as weaving, ceramics, and working with precious metals to the highest level of perfection. This French anthropologist holds that it is difficult to argue the inferiority of societies that have made such a great contribution to the Old World: yams, tobacco, cacao, tomato, and many other foodstuffs. The arithmetical concept of zero, known to and applied by the Maya at least five hundred years before it was discovered by Hindu sages, the greater accuracy of the former's calendar, and the advanced political system of the Incas are further aspects mentioned in order to refute evolutionary theory empirically.

Nevertheless, it was in *The Savage Mind* that Lévi-Strauss best developed his theoretical argument. We read in it that the reason why non-Western cultures reached a level of knowledge in several areas superior to its European counterpart lies in the fact that their intellectual development possessed a precision similar to that of scientific disciplines, though it followed different paths. Only detailed and methodical attention to reality enabled the Hanunöo to develop over 150 terms to describe parts and properties of plants; the Pinatubo, among whom more than six hundred named plants have been recorded, possess a complex knowledge of their uses and more than one hundred terms to describe their parts or characteristic features. Lévi-Strauss concludes that such systematically developed knowledge is not acquired for its practical value alone. There are some tribes that count, name, and classify reptiles that will never be part of their diet or used for utilitarian purposes. "From such examples, which we can find everywhere in the world, it might be inferred that animal and plant species are not known because they are useful, but rather that they are pronounced useful and interesting because they are known first."[3] It is a knowledge produced in societies that assign a central place to intellectual activities. Therefore, what distinguishes the "savage mind" from what the author calls the scientific or "domesticated mind" is not a greater capacity to arrange the world rationally or the predominance of intellectual over practical activity; less so is it the case, as some have claimed, that primitive

knowledge is the result of discoveries made by chance. No one has yet
dared to account for the Neolithic Revolution—such complex activities
as pottery, weaving, farming, and the domestication of animals—in
terms of the fortuitous accumulation of casual discoveries. "Every one
of these skills presupposes centuries of active and methodical observation, bold and controlled hypotheses, to be refuted or confirmed through
assiduously repeated experiences."[4]

Instead of contrasting magic and science, mythical and rational
thought, as if the former were but a clumsy draft of the latter, they should
be placed "side by side like two modes of knowledge, unequal where
theoretical and practical results are concerned (since, from this point of
view, it is true that science is more successful than magic, though magic
foreshadows science in the sense that it also is sometimes right), but not
because of the kind of mental exercise required by either, and which
differ from each other less by their nature than by the class of phenomena
to which they are applied."[5]

To put it another way: these two types of mind—savage and scientific—do not correspond to higher or lower stages of human development, but to distinct "strategic levels in which nature allows itself to be
tackled by scientific knowledge: one of them roughly adjusted to the
level of perception and imagination, and the other displaced."[6] In the
case of the savage mind, more closely linked to sensibility, "concepts are
submerged in images"; in the modern mind, images, the immediate data
derived from sensibility and their imaginary elaboration, are subordinated to concepts.

The antievolutionism to which this kind of reasoning leads was
stirred up by Lévi-Strauss to the point of denying the possibility of any
unified account of history. On this subject, he draws the most radical
conclusions found in his structural formalism, namely, the subordination of history to structure, of structure to formal knowledge about that
structure, and of knowledge to codification. While every society has its
own peculiarities, it is possible to compare societies because they share
a common social and intellectual logic. Ultimately, magic and science
presuppose similar mental exercises; myths or kinship are constructed
from analogous structures. The coincidence lies in synchronic logic
rather than convergent processes, whereby Lévi-Strauss believes that in
establishing a relation between different cultures it is more appropriate
to spread them out in space instead of arranging them in time. Progress
is neither necessary nor continuous; rather, it moves by leaps, not always
in the same direction. As an alternative to the evolutionism borrowed by
history and anthropology from nineteenth-century biology, Lévi-Strauss
puts forward alternative schemes based on probability, chance, and
necessity notions of contemporary physics and biology. He suggests

historical development should be conceived after the fashion of the knight in the game of chess, which has many optional moves open to it all the time, but never in the same direction. Humanity in progress does not resemble a character climbing stairs, adding with each movement a new rung to those already conquered; it conjures up the image of the player whose chances are divided up among many dice, and who, with every throw, sees them scatter on the table, a different outcome each time. What is gained in one hand is always liable to be lost in the next, and only from time to time is history cumulative, that is to say, outcomes add up to create a favorable combination.[7]

Cultural Relativism or Critique of Inequality?

Can this theory of history account for differences between traditional and modern cultures? Can we understand why so often these differences turn into inequalities, or are created by them? It is odd that, despite its theoretical and methodological distance from functionalism and culturalism, despite its effort not to repeat their naïveté, the philosophical and political implications of Lévi-Strauss's structuralism are similar to theirs. British anthropologists (Malinowski, Radcliffe-Brown, Evans-Pritchard) studied archaic societies from a perspective that sought to understand their intrinsic goals. Each society was conceived as a system of institutions and "mechanisms of cooperation intended to meet social needs" (Lucy Mair),[8] whose functioning is coherent if analyzed in its own terms and tends to survive because it is functional. Unlike British thinkers, who believed in the universality and profound similarity of institutions on the basis that they represent responses to universal needs (for sexual desire there is the family, for hunger there is economic organization, for anxiety there is religion), Ruth Benedict maintained that institutions are merely empty forms whose universality is insignificant because every society fills them differently. Anthropologists must focus on this concrete diversity, and, instead of concerning themselves with comparison between cultures, they should study their peculiarities. Herskovits concluded that this plurality of social organization and experiences, each with its own meaning, inhibits our capacity to make judgments from the standpoint of an alien value system. All ethnocentrism has to be dismissed, and we must acknowledge cultural relativism: every society has the right to develop autonomously, without there being a universal theory of humanity that might be imposed on another on the grounds of any kind of superiority.

Two issues remain unresolved. One is of an epistemological nature: how can a universally valid body of knowledge that surpasses the peculiarities of each culture be constructed without representing the imposition of the norms of one society over the rest? The second is of a political nature: how can supracultural criteria of coexistence and interaction be established in a world that is increasingly interrelated through conflict?

In 1947, in view of the "large number of societies which have come into close contact with the modern world and the diversity of their ways of life," the American Anthropological Association put before the United Nations a proposal for a Declaration on the Rights of Man, which aimed to answer the following question: "How can the proposed declaration be applied to all human beings and at the same time not represent a declaration of rights conceived solely in terms of the values dominant in Western Europe and the United States?" Guided by "research in the human sciences," three points of agreement were suggested:

> 1) Individuals realize their personality through culture; respect for individual differences therefore implies respect for cultural differences; 2) Respect for this difference between cultures is validated by the scientific fact that no method has been developed to evaluate cultures qualitatively . . . The goals which guide the life of a society are self-evident in their meaning to that society and cannot be surpassed by any other perspective, including that of eternal pseudotruths; 3) Norms and values are relative to the culture from which they are derived, so that all attempts to formulate postulates derived from beliefs or moral codes from a particular culture must to this extent be withdrawn from the application of any Declaration of the Rights of Man to the whole of humanity.[9]

It is amusing to note how often their proposal, which seeks to avoid ethnocentrism, becomes its victim; how often its claimed scientific basis represents tendentious ideological argumentation. Its starting point is the individual—placed there by classical liberalism—rather than social structure or solidarity or equality among men and women, as other scientific or political theories would maintain. Respect for differences is protected because no method to evaluate cultures qualitatively has been developed, whereupon this line of reasoning is caught within a methodological opposition (quantitative/qualitative) characteristic of Western knowledge.

Besides negating the announced respect for what each culture regards as valuable for itself, the contemptuous attack on myth and religion ("eternal pseudotruths") reveals the extent to which this declaration relies on an empiricist conception that is not even upheld by all Western epistemologies. Last, how can a body of scientific knowledge, which transcends the partial, ethnocentric truths of individual cultures, be constructed from this relativistic skepticism? And how can a policy suitable to the degree of global interdependence already prevalent in the world and to worldwide homogenization attained by imperialist policies be formulated, if we can only count on a pluralism based on voluntaristic or proclaimed respect and indifferent to concrete causes of diversity and inequality between cultures?

Lévi-Strauss's starting point is structure, not the individual; he does not sanctify empiricist evaluations as the sole method of proof, nor does he approach myths with the insensitivity of so many positivist anthropologists. Nevertheless, his search for a multicentered conception of history—which would be correct if it took into account interrelations and conflicts—"interprets" differences as products of chance, with the triviality of someone who scatters dice on a gambling table. Perhaps his other metaphor, that of "the knight in the game of chess, which has many optional moves open to it all the time, but never in the same direction," might have led him, given the political implications of the game, to ask himself whether the choice of one or other direction in social development might not depend on whoever is moving the knights and the pawns. However, on this point the structuralist theory of society is too much like culturalism and functionalism; the former's synchronic omnidetermination of the structure is not far removed from the latter's consensus theory and harmonious interdependence of functions. Thus, all three become useless for conceptualizing changes and conflicts. Liberal thought plays chess with different pieces and a series of strategies, but it cleverly manages to bring functionalism, culturalism, and structuralism together in the end "to create a favorable combination."

The Globalization of Culture

For a long time, it was thought that cultural relativism was the philosophical and political conclusion best suited to the discovery that there are no higher or lower cultures. We have seen that, while it helps to transcend ethnocentrism, it leaves certain fundamental problems of a theory of culture unanswered, namely, the creation of a universally valid body of thought and of criteria that can help to conceptualize and solve conflicts and inequalities between cultures.

Ultimately, cultural relativism founders because it rests on an atomized and naïve conception of power: it pictures each culture existing with no knowledge of others, as if the world were a vast museum of self-sufficient economies, each one in its own display case, unruffled by the proximity of others, invariably reenacting its own codes, its own internal relations. The limited usefulness of cultural relativism is demonstrated when we consider that it gave rise to a new attitude toward remote cultures, but it carries no weight when the "primitives" constitute the "backward" sectors of our own society, those customs and beliefs in the suburbs of our own cities that are alien to us.

The anthropologist's most common task in this era of worldwide capitalist expansion is not to design sanitary cordons between cultures but to find out what happens when cultural relativism is rejected on a daily basis, when people must choose between antagonistic customs and values, when an Indian community feels that capitalism turns its traditional *fiestas* into tourists shows, or when the mass media persuade workers in a city of fifteen million that rural, Indian symbols, as defined by the mass media themselves, represent their identity.

Statements on the equality of all human beings, the relativity of cultures, and the right of every one of them to shape itself are inconsistent unless we consider them within the context of present conditions of globalization and interdependence. In the contemporary world, this interdependence is not a relation of egalitarian reciprocity, as in archaic societies where subsistence exchange was regulated by principles that restored balance time and time again. The nationalization of capital, together with the globalization of culture, imposes an unequal exchange of material and symbolic goods. Even the most remote ethnic groups are forced to subordinate their economic and cultural organization to national markets, and the latter become metropolitan satellites, in accordance with monopoly logic.

The diversity of cultural norms, of consumer goods and habits, is an element that creates intolerable upheaval for the capitalist system's needs to expand constantly. As all forms of production (manual and industrial, rural and urban) are assimilated into a unified system, various forms of cultural production (bourgeois and proletarian, rural and urban) are combined, and to some extent homogenized. The homogenization of expectations does not mean that resources are equalized. The distance between classes and between societies on the fundamental question—ownership and control of the means of production—does not disappear, but a dream is created that everyone can, actually or potentially, enjoy the superiority of the dominant culture. Subordinate cultures are not allowed any autonomous or alternative development, and their production and consumption as well as social structure and language are reorganized in order to make them receptive to capitalist modernization. As the analysis in the following chapters will show, at times the survival of traditional *fiestas* is tolerated, but their nature as communal celebrations becomes weakened amid the commercial organization of tourists' leisure; some artisanal production is allowed to continue, even encouraged, in order to provide additional income for peasant families and thus lessen the numbers of those who migrate to the cities—in other words, in order to "find a solution" to the level of unemployment and injustice created by capitalism, to whose commercial logic the design and circulation of crafts are also subjected.

What is the point, in this context, of talking of cultural relativism? The practical "transcendence" of ethnocentrism brought about by capitalism amounts to the imposition of its own economic and cultural norms on dependent societies and popular classes. In the light of this situation, it is hard to believe in appeals to respect the peculiarities of individual cultures and at the same time renounce those forms of ethnocentrism that hinder harmonious coexistence with others. There are really two types of ethnocentrism in the process of capitalist unequal exchange: an imperial ethnocentrism, which, through the multinationalization of economy and culture, tends to destroy any social organization that turns out to be useless to its interests, and the ethnocentrism of oppressed nations, classes, and *etnias* (ethnic enclaves) that can free themselves only through the emphatic self-affirmation of their economic sovereignty and cultural identity. For the latter, cultural relativism, in its positive aspects, represents the philosophical conclusion to be drawn from the body of knowledge produced by the social sciences as well as a political requirement essential to the development of their own and their independent growth. Hence, to overestimate one's own culture—as nationalist, ethnic, and class movements involved in liberation struggles do—does not always constitute prejudice or a mistake to be regretted; it is in several cases a necessary stage of rejection of the dominant culture and an affirmation of their own. The irrational elements that are part of these processes, the chauvinist temptation, can be controlled in two ways: through self-criticism from within their own culture and through solidaristic interaction with other subordinate groups and nations. A greater universalization of knowledge, free from all ethnocentrism, will come about only when contradictions and inequalities are overcome. As Gramsci maintained, to put an end to the distorting elements of ethnocentrism, "to free oneself from partisan and fallacious ideologies . . . is not a starting point but a point of arrival"; the necessary struggle for objectivity "is the same struggle for the unification of the human race."[10] However, even in such a utopian state, when inequalities die out, a noncontradictory diversity of languages, customs, and cultures will remain.

Toward a Theory of Cultural Production

There are two drawbacks to the widest-ranging concept of culture, one that defines it in opposition to nature, which lead us to reject it. We have already mentioned that, while its use leads to the recognition of all cultures as equal, it does not provide us with the tools to conceptualize their inequalities. On the other hand, it lumps together, under the name of culture, all instances and patterns of behavior of a social formation—economic organization, social relations, intellectual structures, artistic practices—without establishing a hierarchy with the relative weight of each element. As Roger Establet remarked, the notion of culture thus becomes the idealistic synonym of the concept of social formation.[11] Such is the case of anthropologists like Ruth Benedict, for whom culture constitutes the form of society held together by its dominant values.

For these reasons, we prefer to limit the use of the term *culture* to *the production of phenomena that contribute, through symbolic representation or reelaboration of material structures, to understand, reproduce, or transform the social system, in other words, all practices and institutions involved in the administration, renewal, and restructuring of meaning.*

This restriction resembles the one observed by Linton and other anthropologists when they contrast culture and society: they apply the word *culture* only to the realm of beliefs, values, and ideas, excluding technology, the economy, and all behavior that can be empirically observed. However, our definition does not identify the cultural realm with the ideal realm, nor the social with the material; less so does it presume that they can be analyzed separately. On the contrary, ideal processes (of symbolic representation or reelaboration) are linked to material structures, to mechanisms of social reproduction or change, and to practices and institutions that, while engaged primarily with culture, also involve some material elements. Furthermore: all production of meaning is anchored in material structures.

We might also point out the similarity between our definition of culture and the Marxist concept of ideology. Indeed, the theory of culture coincides in part with the theory of ideology, and necessitates it, when it links cultural processes to social conditions of production. Nevertheless, not every aspect of cultural phenomena is ideological, if we assume that a distinctive feature of ideology, according to most Marxist thinkers, is a distortion of reality created by class interests. We have kept the term *culture*, instead of replacing it with that of *ideology*, precisely to include facts in a wider sense. All production of meaning (philosophy, art, science itself) can be explained in relation to its social determinations. But such an explanation does not exhaust the phenomenon in question. Culture does not just represent society; it also fulfills, within the context of the requirements of the production of meaning, the functions of reelaborating social structures and inventing new ones. In addition to *representing* relations of production, it contributes to their *reproduction, transformation,* and *invention.*

Some writers, whose contributions will be used in the following pages, have elaborated, as part of the Marxist theory of ideology, on this function of culture as a means of social reproduction and change. Nevertheless, we prefer to emphasize the difference between culture and ideology, since the interpretation of the latter as a distorted representation of reality remains prevalent in the available bibliography.

What are the methodological consequences of analyzing culture as a system of production? The (still inadequate) development of a theory of symbolic or cultural production enables us to make, in this area, the break with idealism that the social sciences have already carried out at other levels. We will limit to a few pages the account of the threefold movement involved by this reorganization of the theory of culture.

To state that culture is a social process of production is, primarily, to object to conceptions of culture as a spiritual act (expression, creation) or as a manifestation that is alien, external, and subsequent to the relations of production (a simple representation of them). Today we can understand why culture constitutes a specific instance of the social system and at the same time why it cannot be studied in isolation. This is because not only is culture *determined* by the social, defined as distinct from culture, and external to it, but also because it is *part* of every socioeconomic fact. Any practice is simultaneously economic and symbolic; as we act through it, it becomes a representation and we attribute a meaning to it. Buying a dress or commuting to work, two everyday socioeconomic practices, are charged with symbolic meaning: the dress or means of transport—in addition to their use value: to cover ourselves, to go somewhere—signifies our belonging to a particular social class, depending on the fabric and design of the dress, whether we travel by bus or car, the model, and so forth. The features of dress or car tell something about our social place, or the one we would like to have, about what we wish to let others know by our wearing it or using it to get somewhere. Conversely, any cultural fact—attending a concert, preparing a lecture—always leads to an implicit socioeconomic level: I will be paid for the lecture, when we go to the concert we buy tickets to pay for the performance, and, furthermore, those facts link us to the people we work with in a different way than if we were to tell them that we had been to a rock concert or watched a performance of Indian dances.

The difficulties concerning the question of how to relate structure and superstructure arose from the fact that *difference* was conceived as *separation*. In reality, economy and culture march along intertwined with one another. They may be distinguished at the level of theoretical/methodological instances and separated at the level of scientific representation, but this necessary differentiation at the analytic moment of knowledge—with a certain basis on appearances—must be overcome in a synthesis that provides an account of their integration. The *unity* and *difference* of levels that make up the social totality must be taken into account at the same time. No scientific knowledge of superstructures is possible unless they are distinguished from the economic base, and we can analyze the ways in which they are determined by the base: at a different rate and with different effectiveness on political ideologies, family ethics, or literature. However, while we should determine the specificity of each individual instance in order to detect its own process, we must not overlook their reciprocal dependence, or else the meaning that proceeds from the totality of which they are part will be lost.

The study of both archaic and capitalist societies has shown that the economic and cultural realms form an indivisible whole. Any process of material production includes, from its very beginning, active ideal elements necessary for the development of the infrastructure. Thought is not a simple reflection of productive forces: it is in them, from the beginning, an internal condition of their emergence. For there to be a tractor or a computer, material facts that gave rise to significant changes in the development of forces and relations of production, it was necessary for engineers first to develop a concept of a tractor or computer before either took on a material form; which is not to say that they sprang up solely from intellectual constructions, that the ideal world generates the material one, because a degree of development of the material base and social forces was in turn necessary for those machines to be conceived. Similarly, kinship relations or relations of production cannot be changed without at the same time defining new rules concerning lineage, marriage, and property, which do not constitute *a posteriori* representations of changes but component elements of the process that must be present from the beginning. This ideal element, present in all material development, is not, then, simply the contents of consciousness; it exists at the same time within social relations, which are therefore also relations of signification or meaning.[12]

Second, to talk of culture as production presupposes taking into consideration material and productive processes necessary to create, know, or represent something. In a general sense, the production of culture grows out of the global needs of a social system and is determined by it. More specifically, there exists a material organization appropriate for each cultural production, making its existence possible (universities for knowledge, publishing houses for books, etc.). The study of these institutions and of the social conditions established by them for the development of cultural products is crucial if we are to understand them. By recognizing the significance of these intermediary structures, we avoid two methodological distortions: studying cultural products, such as a play or a popular dance, concentrating only on the internal meaning of the particular work, as an idealist critique would do, or simplistically relating the structure of the play to society as a whole. Between the general social determinations and each individual cultural product there is an intermediate area, a theater production in one instance, a dance production in another. Although the same society is involved, the social organization within which plays are created differs from the one that promotes popular dances. The general determinations that capitalism exercises over artistic production are mediated by the structure of the world of theater, in one case, and by the structure of those groups or institutions that organize dances, on the other.

Therefore, the analysis must proceed at two levels. On the one hand, it must consider cultural products as *representations*: how social conflicts are staged in a play or choreographed in a dance, which classes are represented, how the formal processes of particular languages are used to present their own perspective; in this case, there is a relationship between social *reality* and ideal *representation*. On the other hand, the analysis must link the *social structure* with the *structure of the world of theater* and with the *structure of the world of dance*, meaning, by the structure of each world, social relations that stage artists and dancers maintain with other elements of the aesthetic processes: means of production (materials, methods) and social relations of production (with the public, with those who provide financing, with official organisms, etc.).[13]

Third, the study of culture as production implies taking into account not only the act of production but every step in a productive process: *production, circulation,* and *reception.* This is another way of saying that the analysis of a particular culture cannot focus on cultural objects or goods; it must concern itself with the process of production and social circulation of objects and meanings that different recipients attribute to them. A dance about Moors and Christians performed by Indians in their community and for themselves *is* not the same dance when it is performed in an urban theater before an audience alien to that tradition, though the formal structures might be identical. This will become even clearer in chapter 4, with regard to crafts: pots made by Indian communities following the principles of manual production and the prevalence of use value in what are virtually self-sufficient economies are then sold in urban markets in accordance with their exchange value and eventually bought by foreign tourists for their aesthetic value. Only a global vision of this process can explain the meaning of this production, torn from its social course.

Culture, Social Reproduction, and Power

The second theoretical event that, together with an analysis of production, helps to place culture within the context of socioeconomic development is the one that regards culture as a means for social reproduction and struggle for hegemony. The origins of this current of thought can be traced back to Marx, but it was Gramsci who gave such concepts a central role in his reflections on culture. The elaboration of his conjectures by recent authors (Angelo Broccoli, Christine Buci-Glucksmann), together with the works of Althusser, Baudelot, and Establet, has shown how fruitful this line of thought is for Marxist analyses, particularly in the area of education. Under a strong Marxist influence, creatively related to other sociological trends (especially Weber), Pierre Bourdieu has taken this model to its highest systematization and has demonstrated its explanatory power in two fundamental books: those that deal, respectively, with the educational system and with the production, circulation, and consumption of artistic goods.[14]

In order to survive, social systems must reproduce and reformulate their conditions of production. Every social formation reproduces its labor force through wages and its skills through education, and, last, it constantly reproduces workers' assimilation to the social order through an ideological-cultural policy that governs their entire life at work, with their families, and during leisure, so that every aspect of their behavior and relations will have a meaning compatible with the dominant social organization. The reproduction of assimilation to the social order necessitates the "reproduction of [their] submission to the dominant ideology where workers are concerned and the reproduction of their capacity to manage ideology properly where agents of exploitation are concerned."[15]

It should be added that it also requires the reassimilation of workers to changes in the dominant ideology and the social system, and a renewal—not just reproduction—of the dominant ideology in response to changes in the productive system and social conflicts. (I believe that this adjunct is essential to overcome the static nature of Althusser's conception of ideology, particularly as formulated in his earlier texts.)

Through the reproduction of adaptation, the dominant class seeks to create and renew mass consensus over a policy that protects its economic privileges. A full hegemonic policy requires the following: (1) ownership of the means of production and the capacity to appropriate surplus value; (2) control of all mechanisms necessary for material and symbolic reproduction of the labor force and the relations of production (wages, schooling, mass media, and other institutions that can train workers and generate consensus); and (3) control of coercive mechanisms (military, police, and other repressive apparatuses) through which ownership of the means of production and continuity in the appropriation of surplus value can be safeguarded when consensus drops or is lost.

Ownership of the means of production and the capacity to appropriate the surplus are the basis of all hegemony. However, the hegemony of a class cannot sustain itself in any society solely through economic power. At the other extreme, we find mechanisms of repression that, through surveillance, intimidation, or punishment, guarantee—as a last resort—the submission of subordinate classes. But this is only as a *last* resort. No hegemonic class can ensure its economic power for a long period of time through the sole use of repressive power. Cultural power plays a key role between them: (1) it imposes ideological-cultural norms that prepare members of society for an arbitrary economic and political structure (arbitrary in the sense that there are no biological, social, or "spiritual" reasons, derived from a supposedly "human nature" or "order of things," which make a particular social structure necessary); (2) it legitimates the dominant structure, which is seen as *the* "natural" form of social organization and thus conceals its arbitrariness; and (3) it also covers up the violence involved in the assimilation of individuals to structures set up without their participation and makes the imposition of such structures appear as the level of socialization or assimilation necessary to live in society (and not in a preconceived society). Thus, cultural power not only reproduces sociocultural arbitrariness but also represents such arbitrariness as necessary and natural; it conceals economic power and aids the exercise and perpetuation of such power.

The effectiveness of this imposition-dissimulation of sociocultural arbitrariness is based, in part, on the global power of the dominant class and on the possibility of enforcing it through the state, a system of apparatuses that represents in part—although it claims to represent fully—not one particular class but society as a whole. A further consideration is the fact that the state increasingly extends its organization and control over all aspects of social life: economic, political, cultural, and everyday existence. However, the degree of effectiveness rests, at the same time, on the need of individuals to be socialized and to assimilate to some kind of social structure that will allow their self-development and will satisfy their need for emotional security. That is why the realization that the social organization of which we are part and the habits acquired in it are arbitrary and relative in nature is always a belated and secondary perception. Even more so is the critique of such organization and habits. Pierre Bourdieu is right when he argues that

it is one thing to teach cultural relativism, i.e., the arbitrary nature of all culture, to individuals who have already been educated according to the principles of cultural arbitrariness of particular groups or classes; it would be a very different matter to expect to provide a relativistic education, i.e., to produce a cultured individual who was a native of all cultures. The problems posed by situations of precocious bilingualism or biculturalism offer only a glimpse of the unsolvable contradiction which any pedagogical action seeking to adopt the theoretical affirmation of the arbitrariness of linguistic or cultural codes as a practical principle of learning, would encounter.[16]

The difficulty to perceive one's own culture as relative and the tendency to make absolute the semantic universe in which we live have tremendous significance for any political action that seeks to bring about change. How can the distancing necessary for the growth of a critical outlook vis-à-vis those patterns of life imposed upon us but assimilated by us as if they were our own be brought about? And, second, how can we create a sustained critical discipline, how can we prevent the alternative ideology with which we thrust change—progressive Catholicism, ethnocentric nationalism, or a version of socialism formulated according to conjunctural exigencies—from becoming a self-contained, enclosed system and therefore with a tendency to resist its own self-renewal? This is one of the toughest problems concerning the political role of popular cultures, but we would be deluding ourselves if we confined it to the "less educated" sectors. Certainly, the development of the critical powers of the masses and their actual participation are crucial to its solution. However, history shows us that it also represents a risk for intellectuals and revolutionary political leaders, because increased practice and intellectual openness to critical thinking do not automatically lead to freedom from the centripetal and self-justifying tendency of all cultural systems.

Everyday Organization of Domination

A despotic order consolidates itself when it creates its own mirror image within the realm of subjectivity. From Freud to Deleuze, from Nietzsche to Foucault, we have been told that oppression cannot exist in the anonymity of collective structures alone: it feeds on the echo that the social world generates within individuals. Psychoanalysis, and its detractors, have developed concepts to understand this internalization of the social order, but mostly from the viewpoint of the subject (even though it might be a decentered, disputed subject, one pierced by objective structures). How can this process be understood in sociological terms? What can Marxism say about it? Bourdieu has put forward an analytical model that brings together economic, sociological, and psychological concepts, articulated through a vast body of theoretical and empirical research: it seeks to understand how a particular cultural capital is passed on through a variety of apparatuses, giving rise to cultural habitus and practices.

Liberal theories of education perceive it as a set of institutional mechanisms that ensure the transfer of inherited culture from generation to generation. The implicit postulate of such theories is that various pedagogical actions practiced in a social formation work together harmoniously to reproduce a *cultural capital* that is regarded as common property. And yet, Bourdieu objects, cultural goods accumulated throughout the history of every society do not *really* belong to all (though they might be formally offered to all), but to those who possess means to appropriate them. To understand a scientific text or to enjoy a piece of music, a person must have access to certain codes, intellectual training, and the development of a particular sensitivity necessary to decipher them. Since the educational system gives some individuals and denies others—depending on their socioeconomic status—the resources required to appropriate cultural capital, the structure of education reproduces the existing structure of its distribution among classes.

Cultural apparatuses are those institutions that administer, transfer, and renew cultural capital. Under capitalism, they are primarily the family and education, but they also include the mass media, forms of organization of space and time, and all material institutions and structures through which meaning is carried (we will study the influence of state cultural apparatuses on changing crafts in chap. 3 and the various spaces through which they pass—the Indian household, the market, the urban shop, etc.—in chap. 5). Let us say for now that in noncapitalist societies—or wherever enclaves of noncapitalist forms of life survive—these functions are usually combined with others of an economic and social nature; very rarely are there separate institutions for cultural development, and the latter takes place within the process of production itself or through institutions that combine both economic and cultural elements (e.g., systems of kinship, *cargos*, or *mayordomías*).

But the action of cultural apparatuses must be internalized by members of society, and the objective organization of culture needs to shape each subjectivity. This internalization of structures of meaning generates *habitus* (i.e., systems of aptitudes and basic schemes of perception, understanding, and action). Habitus are both structured (by social conditions and class position) and structuring (generators of practices and schemes of perception and appreciation): the combination of these two faculties present in habitus constitutes what Bourdieu has called "life style." It is habit that makes a set of practices by a person or group both systematic and systematically distinct from those practices that constitute a different life-style. In other words, the cultural apparatuses in which every class participates—schools, for example—generate different aesthetic habitus, different structures of taste that will make some individuals prefer high art and others crafts.

Finally, from habitus come *practices*, to the extent that subjects who have internalized them find themselves in positions, in the class structure, conducive to the realization of such habitus. There is a correspondence, then, between the possibilities of appropriating economic capital and cultural capital. Comparable socioeconomic conditions lead to similar educational levels and cultural institutions, and ways of thinking and feeling acquired in them in turn generate distinctive cultural practices.

Tasks for Future Research

We have briefly gone over several points of intersection between Marxism, anthropology, and sociology, but there are other aspects central to a theory of culture that remain to be discussed. Not least important among these are contributions made by semiotics to explain processes of signification and by psychoanalysis to account for unconscious processes of symbolization and sublimation that are at the heart of cultural production. Nevertheless, at present we will mention only some of the consequences that this line of analysis might have for social research in Latin America.

1. The formulation of a scientific theory of culture is essential to the development of social sciences, not only as a complement to economic analysis in order to avoid economic reductionism, but also to understand the economic structure itself, of which symbolic phenomena are a part. The unity and interdependence between structure and superstructure—demonstrated, as we have already seen, at the theoretical level—are particularly significant on our continent, given the role played by ethnic and cultural conflicts in social movements. How can we understand our present history if we approach key issues such as the incorporation of traditional forms of (Indian) peasant production into the capitalist system from the purely economic question of whether we are dealing with a situation of articulation or subsumption, if we do not include the struggle for symbolic hegemony as part of the conflict or contemptuously relegate it to culturalistic polemics between *indigenismo* and its opponents? Perhaps in Latin America there are additional reasons to reevaluate the role of cultural factors in class differentiation and conflict—a role that Marx and Lenin had themselves acknowledged and which several European Marxists (Edward P. Thompson, Nicos Poulantzas, etc.), without forgetting the determinant role of relations of production, have elaborated further in recent years. Though much remains to be done on the interaction between economic and cultural phenomena in our reality, it is clear that identity changes experienced by migrant workers and acculturated Indians and mestizos as well as their

new location within the process of capitalist development cannot be explained solely by the extraction of surplus value: their exploitation is organized around, and rests on, multiple mechanisms that are not always so apparent if we search for them within the realm of production rather than consumption, in the dispossession of the means of production alone instead of in their relation to language, health, or the system of beliefs.

2. Hence arises the need to encourage research on forms of circulation and appropriation of cultural capital in Latin America and its role in the reproduction and transformation of the social system. Apart from the fact that Bourdieu's model is in need of a degree of historicity (which will lead to the recognition that instead of being entirely arbitrary, bourgeois culture is the product of a particular development of forces of production and social relations), it must be made more specific, in accordance with the stages in which a heterogeneous cultural capital, the product of the convergence of several contributions, came into being in our continent: (1) the legacy from the great pre-Columbian cultures, whose customs, languages, and systems of thought survive in Mexico, Central America, and the Andean high plateau; (2) European migration, particularly from Spain and Portugal; and (3) the African presence in Brazil, Colombia, and the Caribbean.[17] We need to determine how the combination and interpenetration of these cultural capitals have shaped our identity and what the strategies of accumulation and renewal of each particular one have been. This book seeks to establish how these cultural capitals relate to each other in today's class conflicts: how the Indian legacy and peasant and urban popular cultures are appropriated by dominant and subordinate sectors, and how they become recontextualized and invested with new meaning to serve the interests of these various sectors; also, how the multinational logic of culture under capitalism molds habitus and practices, forms of conciousness and life, and what our societies can do to appropriate their lost or expropriated cultural capital, to renew it in response to current tasks.

The importance of more studies to understand the needs of Latin American societies (what constitutes *our* art, *our* medicine, *our* education today?), to determine within which particular cultural apparatuses we must fight or where we can set up alternative ones, how to wage this struggle in the area of subjectivity in order to create new habitus and practices that will bring about change, should be obvious.

2. Introduction to the Study of Popular Cultures

Definition of the Popular: Romanticism, Positivism, and the Gramscian Tendency

Following our earlier discussion, how can we formulate a concept of popular culture? First of all, popular culture must not be taken as the "expression" of the personality of a particular people, as idealism does, because such a personality does not exist as a metaphysical a priori entity, and comes into being as a result of the interaction of social relations. Nor is it a set of ideal traditions or essences, ethereally preserved: cultural production, as we have seen, emerges from material living conditions and is rooted in them. This is very clearly shown in the case of popular classes, where songs, beliefs, and *fiestas* are more closely linked on a daily basis to those material tasks that consume virtually all of their time. For that very reason, it does not seem useful, in order to account for popular cultural processes, to conceptualize them either as empty forms universally found, as functionalism does, or as mental logical processes that will adopt particular types in different contexts, as structuralism does.

Popular cultures (rather than popular culture) are formed through a process of unequal appropriation of the economic and cultural property of a nation or ethnic group by some of its subordinate sectors, and through both a symbolic and real understanding, reproduction, and transformation of general as well as particular living and working conditions.

We have already discussed relations between economic and cultural capital, as well as the fact that ownership or otherwise of economic capital gives rise to unequal participation in educational capital and therefore in the appropriation of cultural property available in a particular society. However, the peculiarity of popular cultures does not derive solely from the fact that the appropriation of what society has is smaller and different; it also derives from the fact that the people create at work, and in their lives in general, specific forms of representation, reproduction, and symbolic reelaboration of their social relations. In the previous chapter, we examined the sense in which culture is representation, production, reproduction, and symbolic reelaboration. At this point, we must add that the people carry out these processes while participating in the general conditions of production, circulation, and consumption of the system in which they live (e.g., a dependent social formation) and at the same time by creating their own structures. Therefore, popular cultures are constituted within two spaces: (1) labor, familial, communication, and all other kinds of practices through which the capitalist system organizes the life of all its members; and (2) practices and forms of thought that popular sectors create for themselves, to conceptualize and express their own reality, their own subordinate role in the spheres of production, circulation, and consumption. In a sense, what owner and worker have in common is their participation in the same job in the same factory, the fact that they watch the same television channels (though, of course, from distinct positions that generate different decodifications); but at the same time, there are economic and cultural options that differentiate them, as well as separate jargons and channels of communication peculiar to each class. Both spaces, that of hegemonic culture and that of popular culture, interpenetrate each other, such that the particular language of workers or peasants is partly original construction, partly reformulation of the language of the mass media and political power, or a specific mode of referring to social conditions shared by all (e.g., jokes on inflation). A similar interaction exists in the opposite direction too: the hegemonic language of the mass media or politicians will incorporate popular forms of expression to the extent that it wants to reach the entire population.

In short, popular cultures are the product of *unequal appropriation* of cultural capital, the *people's own reflections* about their living conditions, and *conflict-ridden interaction* with hegemonic sectors. Thus understood, their analysis can move away from the two positions that have prevailed until now: immanent interpretations, formulated in Europe by romantic populism and in Latin America by conservative nationalism and *indigenismo,* on the one hand, and positivism, which, concerned with scientific precision, ignored the political meaning of symbolic production among the people, on the other.

Romantics regarded the people as a homogeneous and autonomous whole, whose spontaneous creativity represented the highest expression of human values and the way of life to which humanity should return. Belief in popular culture as the authentic repository of human nature and the true essence of the nation, set apart from the artificial meaning of a "civilization" that denied its existence, was somewhat useful to vindicate popular thought and customs, to stimulate its study and protection after a long absence from academic learning. However, such exaltation was based on sentimental enthusiasm, which could not be kept up when positivist philology showed that what the people produced—it was referring particularly to the case of poetry—came out of both the direct experience of popular classes and their contact with "high" art and thought, that their existence derived to a considerable degree from a "degraded absorption" of the dominant culture.[1]

Romantic idealization, into which hardly any scholar dares fall any longer, still attracts many folklorists and *indigenistas* in Latin America, and it continues to be used within nationalist political discourse. Though not always influenced by European romanticism, they fall back onto many of its hypotheses. This metaphysical vision of the people imagines them as the place where virtues of a biological (appertaining to race) and irrational character (love for the land, religion, and ancestral beliefs) would be preserved untouched. Overvaluing biological and telluric components, characteristic of right-wing thinking, helps bourgeois nationalist populism identify its interests with those of the nation, and conceal its dependence on imperialism and, internally, any class conflicts that threaten its privileges. The historical dynamic that formed the concept and sense of nationhood is neutralized and diluted in "tradition." From this concept of folklore as a fossilized and apolitical archive, a populist policy is promoted that, under the pretext of "giving the people what they like," avoids worrying itself with whether popular culture develops by being offered canned goods or the right to choose and create. Nor is the question posed as to who does the giving, or who, through centuries of domination, shaped their taste.

For many university scholars, the scientific alternative to this idealization is empiricism, more or less positivistic. They urge direct contact with reality, careful and detailed study of objects and customs, and their classification by ethnic origin and immediately observable differences. This alternative form of passion, governed by analytical precision but fascinated by the neglected worth of oppressed ethnic enclaves to the point of spending many years in a small village to record even the most minute detail, has produced monographs and books of great value for understanding myths, legends, ceremonies, crafts, customs, and institutions. However, we have to ask ourselves why there is an imbalance in most of these works between the data gathered and the conclusions that have been reached. It seems that this results from a narrow focus on the object studied—they look only at crafts or at the local community—and its misconceived role within the process of development of capitalism.

The drawbacks of this approach did not disappear as attempts were made to account for changes in the identity of traditional societies through a theory of "culture contact." Such studies, launched in the thirties with the early works on acculturation by the American Social Science Research Council[2] and the publication in the United Kingdom of *Methods of Study of Culture Contact in Africa in 1938*,[3] were not able to overcome the neutral character of the concepts of acculturation and cultural contact and their inability to explain those conflicts and processes of domination they usually involve. With meticulous kind-heartedness, they called the exploiters "givers of values" and the reaction of the oppressed "assimilation." Linton introduced a significant variation when he talked of "guided change" to account for cases in which "a contact group interferes actively or intentionally with the culture of another."[4] But he also failed to situate such interference properly in relation to its socioeconomic causes.

Psychologistic and culturalist interpretations with which anthropologists in the metropolis sought to account for cultural change and local resistance found a mild echo among Latin American anthropologists, particularly those who had had Redfield, Beals, and other ideologues of the theory of "modernization of primitive societies" as teachers. Perhaps Aguirre Beltrán stands out among those who follow this tendency because of his somewhat original reformulation of acculturation phenomena and his influence on *indigenista* policies. Although his works consider forms of domination and the productive foundations of intercultural contacts, they do not assign sufficient weight to material determinations. They overrate ethnicity, which is seen in isolation, and their theoretical and empirical problematic fits the objectives of integration and conciliation that permeate their political project, that is, to construct a "doctrine which guides and explains the methods and goals pursued by *indigenista* action."[5]

We believe that the analysis of intercultural conflicts cannot be guided by a concern either to exalt popular culture or to attach oneself conservatively to the immediate appearance and meaning that the community itself attributes to these facts, nor can it be guided by an interest in making it ready for modernization. The critical issue is to understand popular cultures in relation to conflicts between social classes and to the conditions of exploitation under which those sectors produce and consume.

In fact, when ways of approaching intercultural relations are placed within their political and historical context, their controversial nature becomes clearer. Concern with what has been called cultural contact or acculturation *between different societies* emerged during the imperialist expansion of capitalism and the need to widen the world market at the end of the nineteenth century and beginning of the twentieth. On the other hand, rapid industrialization and urbanization since the forties, with consequent massive migrations and the creation of slums (*ciudades perdidas, villas miserias, favelas)* in large urban centers and capitalist reorganization of the peasant economy and culture, intensified existing contradictions in the countryside, in the city, and between them: out of this process came the concern to understand intercultural conflicts within individual societies and between their different classes and ethnic groups.

However, the failure to explain these processes is not unique to anthropological trends. Marxism, which offers a theory with greater explanatory power regarding such conflicts under capitalism, has not generated much research on the subject either: it has tended to favor the analysis of economic aspects, and on the issue of culture it has concerned itself almost exclusively with the ideology of the dominant classes. Since Gramsci, the popular has gained a new scientific and political place of its own, but only in recent years have some anthropologists, particularly Italian ones, applied his laconic intuitions from prison to empirical research. A first conclusion of these reflections is that the most promising framework for the study of popular cultures can be found at the crossroads of Marxist accounts of the dynamics of capitalism and empirical, and in part methodological, contributions of anthropology and sociology.

It is necessary, in order to define more precisely our own ideas, to mention briefly those aspects in the texts by Gramsci and his followers (Cirese, Lombardi Satriani) that we consider most valuable as well as those that in our view are problematic. We have already applied in the previous chapter one Gramscian contribution that we regard as most fruitful, namely, the connection made between culture and hegemony. His notes were edited and further elaborated by Alberto M. Cirese in a study that constitutes perhaps the most valuable European theoretical contribution on this subject. Cirese rejects those who define popular culture according to some intrinsic qualities or set of characteristics peculiar to it, and denotes it instead in relation to those cultures that oppose it. The popular element in any phenomenon must be established by its use rather than by its origin, "as fact rather than essence, as relational position rather than substance." What constitutes the popular aspect of a cultural fact, he goes on to say, "is the historical relationship, one of difference or contrast, with other cultural facts."[6] However, this *dialectical* conception of social relations is contradicted by his further suggestion of "imbalances" between cultures. He distinguishes two kinds: "external imbalances," that is, those that exist between European societies and "ethnological or primitive" ones, and "internal imbalances" within Western societies, between dominant and subordinate strata in a single social formation. To talk of *levels* at various heights seems too static, implying a concept that can scarcely encompass those *inequalities* and *conflicts* that constantly link popular and hegemonic cultures. The use of terms like these leads him to call those processes involving messages and products as they pass from one level to another "downward" and "upward processes," something which—despite many caveats—connotes an unacceptable hierarchy.

If we look seriously at the "reciprocal exchanges, diffusion and conditionings" beween popular cultures and others to which Cirese himself refers,[7] the concept of imbalance does not seem the most suitable to describe them. On the contrary, compartmentalizing culture into parallel processes, as in some kind of geological stratification, implies giving in to those static classifications so characteristic of classical folklore and against which both Gramsci and Cirese in his most Gramscian texts set up a critical and dynamic analytical strategy. Research cannot focus on imbalance; it must look at inequalities and conflicts between symbolic manifestations of classes that are prevented from becoming autonomous by their joint participation in the same system.

All studies influenced by a Gramscian analytical framework share one problem: the strong emphasis placed on both the opposition between subordinate and hegemonic cultures and the political need to protect the independence of the former leads them to regard both as systems foreign to each other. This is even more clear in the works of Lombardi Satriani, particularly in the way they have been interpreted in Latin America. Hegemonic and subordinate cultures are set in contrast to each other in such a Manichean fashion that "anesthetizing" or "challenging" qualities are too easily attributed to cultural phenomena that are neither one nor the other, but a combination of experiences and representations whose ambiguities correspond to the unresolved nature of contradictions among popular sectors. One cannot deny the value of Lombardi Satriani's thought-provoking analyses of the structure of popular cultures, including their interaction with the dominant culture (e.g., the chapter on "folkmarkets" in *Apropiación y destrucción de la cultura de las clases subalternas*),[8] but his approach is dominated by a categorical opposition between hegemonic and subordinate, which are seen as intrinsic qualities of certain messages rather than forms—ambiguous and temporary—of conflicts binding them together.

For Satriani, the opposition between domination and cultural resistance has an inceptive nature, as if we were dealing with two phenomena foreign to each other, whose existence came before both cultures became part of a single social system. This model might fit the initial processes of colonization, when capitalist expansion brought its own standards in from abroad and Indian communities confronted this imposition as a mass. It is useful to explain the conquest of America by Spaniards and

Portuguese, as well as later stages when the reduction of conflict gave rise to a certain degree of relative autonomy of subjected and dominant cultures. But it cannot be applied to the present development of monopoly capitalism that brings under its control every society it dominates, thus building a dense system in which socioeconomic and cultural conflict *precedes* policies of domination and resistance, and which combines the anesthetizing, challenging, or other uses that products may undergo.

Instead of considering "questioning" and "anesthetizing" phenomena, then, the study should focus on the structure of conflict, which does indeed include the former phenomena, as well as others of integration, interpenetration, concealment, dissimulation, and cushioning of social contradictions. We still lack a typology of interactions between popular and dominant cultures, and the only way to construct one is to carry out research on various processes, as long as such studies include the diversity of existing links between cultures without hastening to classify them according to positive or negative effects.

Finally, why talk of popular cultures? We prefer this term to others used in anthropology, sociology, and folklore—oral, traditional, or subordinate culture—which assume to some extent the possibility of reducing the popular to an essential characteristic. While we might occasionally use the term *traditional* to refer to a certain aspect or type of popular culture that comes into being through opposition to *modernity*, such words must be read in quotation marks (though we may have left them out in order to simplify the text), as formulas used for their functional value, to identify *phenomena*, not essences, that exist and need to be given a name, though they are not determinant. Equally, we will use *subordinate culture* when we wish to emphasize popular culture's opposition to the dominant one. But, in fact, there is no such thing as *an* oral, traditional, or subordinate culture. We agree with Giovanni Battista Bronzini when he writes that

> oral culture, traditionalism, illiteracy, subordination, are phenomena of communication and/or of an economic and social nature, inherent to the structure of society and the system of production . . . As phenomena they do not produce culture, nor do they create sufficient conditions for its production, but they become cultural channels and means of production in given times and places and in certain social situations. Subordination itself is historically differentiated: as socioeconomic condition it smothers culture, as class consciousness it stimulates it. The constant factor in cultural production is the work done by popular classes during phases of oppression and liberation.[9]

Why Crafts and *Fiestas*

I have chosen these two manifestations to examine changes in popular culture under capitalism because artisanal *objects* and the *event* of the *fiesta* are not only fundamental but also reflect, in Indian as well as many mestizo villages, the major conflicts that result from their integration into capitalism to modernization. Through the production, circulation, and consumption of crafts and through changes undergone by *fiestas*, we can study the *economic* function of cultural facts (instruments for social reproduction), their *political* function (fighting for hegemony), and their *psychosocial* functions (to create consensus and identity and to neutralize or work out contradictions at the symbolic level). The complex composition of crafts and *fiestas* and the diversity of social phenomena included in them helps the simultaneous study of culture as it manifests itself in three main areas: *texts, social practices or relations*, and *organization of space*. To talk of crafts requires much more than descriptions of design and methods of production; their meaning can be fully comprehended only when they are considered in relation to texts that predict and promote them (myths and decrees, tourist brochures and conditions for contests), to the social practices of the people who produce and trade them, who look at them or buy them (in a village, a peasant or urban market, a boutique, or a museum), and to the place they occupy together with other objects in the social organization of space (vegetables or antiques, on a dirt floor or behind the seductive cunning of shop windows).

What gives crafts their character: the fact that they are produced by Indians or peasants, by hand and anonymously, their elementary nature, or their traditional iconography? Establishing their identity and boundaries has become more difficult in recent years, because goods considered to be crafts change as they come into contact with the capitalist market, tourism, "cultural industry," "modern" forms of art, communication, and recreation. But it is not just a question of changes in the meaning and function of crafts; this problem is part of a widespread identity crisis felt in contemporary societies. The homogenization of cultural patterns and the grave nature of conflicts between symbolic systems challenges a whole series of assumptions and differences that until now have reassured us: whites on one side, blacks on the other; Westerners over here, Indians over there; art in urban galleries and museums, crafts in the countryside.

Aesthetic stereotypes such as those that distinguished between "high" art and "mass" and popular art have also succumbed. These three systems of representation functioned fairly independently of each other and each one reflected different social classes: high art reflected the interests and tastes of the bourgeoisie and cultured sectors of the petite bourgeoisie, mass art—more accurately described as art for the masses—reflected those of urban middle and proletarian sectors, and crafts reflected those of the peasantry. The distance betwen elitist aesthetic standards and the artistic prowess of subordinate classes expressed, and reaffirmed, the separation between social classes. The dominant sectors had exclusive control over codes of "good taste," as established by themselves, and this served as a status symbol against cultural massification. Art for the masses and folklore both conveyed to popular classes a worldview that legitimized their oppression and vindicated their traditions and customs within a distinct space, where ignorance of "great culture" and inability to understand and enjoy it validated the distance between people and elites. Both came together formally in official speeches and in calls for national unity, but were neatly separated when it came to setting up different organisms for their management, awarding prizes, or representing their country abroad: crafts were entered in competitions of popular art; works of art were sent to exhibitions.

This is still going on to some extent. But many factors conspire against such a rigorous distinction between symbolic systems. Certain factories resort to native designs in their industrial production, and there are artisans who introduce the iconography of high art or the mass media in their works, as is the case of the Zapotec artisans from Teotitlan del Valle, in Oaxaca, who weave *sarapes* (colorful woolen shawls) with images by Klee and Picasso. In urban stores and rural markets, there are both crafts and industrial goods. Multinational record corporations distribute traditional music in metropolises, while the dances with which small peasant villages celebrate their ancient *fiestas* take place to the music of rock groups. We could cite pop art, satirical verses put to commercial music, and the use of peasant images in advertising to suggest the "natural" character of a recently created product, plastic decorations in rural households and hand looms present in modern apartments, as further examples of the way in which aesthetic systems encounter each other and seem to break up into mixed forms of representation and organization of space.[10]

Popular culture, then, cannot be defined, as we have already said, according to some a priori essence; neither can arts and crafts nor *fiestas*: there is no intrinsic element—for example, the fact that they are handmade—that is sufficient, nor can the problem be solved by an accumulation of several such elements.

Recent studies have attempted to define the specificity of crafts from the perspective of economic analysis, taking into account only the labor process (not the meaning that develops through consumption) or the type of economic subordination to capitalism (without considering, however, the role of cultural factors in such characterization).

Nor is it possible to define popular art or culture only in contrast to high or mass art; the starting point must be the system that gives rise to them all, which ascribes a particular place to each one of them, and reorganizes and combines them, in order to fulfill economic, political, and psychosocial functions necessary for its reproduction. Therefore, we need to look at arts and crafts as process rather than outcome,[11] as products that echo social relations rather than self-contained objects.

However, which concept of crafts will we use to make ourselves clear? If we consider the various uses of the term—in official texts and store signs, in colloquial language and tourist guides—we would have to include virtually everything made by hand, in a rudimentary fashion, by Indians and others, with forms that evoke pre-Columbian iconography or simply suggest "oldness" or "primitivism": rush baskets and hats, domestic ceramics and clay sculptures, expensive and rustic silver articles, objects carved by young urban hippies, and others, made and used by peasants, whose aesthetic value is unimportant (*huaraches*, hammocks, etc.).

These articles differ from each other in terms of labor processes, channels of circulation, market value, consumers, and uses and meanings attributed to them by different recipients. It does not seem desirable to confine the term *crafts* to one area of this cosmos before we have set out on our intended theoretical and empirical study. We will provisionally adopt this diversity of meaning and include in our research very different situations when the term is used in ways not immediately compatible: raising questions about this semantic and pragmatic confusion will help us understand the extent and change of their social functions. When we come to the last chapter, we should be in a better position to propose a more rigorous use of the concept of crafts.

We will not talk about *fiestas*, as phenomenologists of religion (Otto, Eliade) and some anthropologists (Duvignaud) do, as a break from routine, a change from the profane to the sacred, a search for a primordial time when "the sacred dimension of life is fully encountered, the sanctity of human existence as divine creation is experienced."[12] On the contrary, I realized through my fieldwork that the *fiesta* reflects the entire life of each community, its economic organization and cultural structures, its political relations and any projects to change them. In a phenomenal sense, it is true that the *fiesta* involves a degree of discontinuity and exceptionality: Indians interrupt regular work (though this is done in order to perform other tasks, sometimes longer and more intense), wear special clothes, and make unusual meals and decorations.

However, I do not feel that all these factors together place the *fiesta* in a time and place set against everyday life.

Peasant *fiestas*, with Indian and colonial roots, and even religious ones of more recent origin, are movements of communal unification to celebrate events or beliefs that *originate* from their daily experience with nature and other individuals (when they are the product of popular initiative) or are *imposed* (by the church or cultural power) to guide the representation of their material living conditions. Often associated with the productive cycle and the rhythm of sowing and harvesting, they are a way to do at the symbolic level, and sometimes to appropriate materially, what a hostile nature or an unjust society denies them, to celebrate that gift, to remember and relive the manner in which they received it in the past, and to search and prepare for its future arrival. Whether they celebrate a recent event (a plentiful harvest) or commemorate distant and mythical ones (the crucifixion and resurrection of Christ), the reason behind the *fiesta* is related to the communal life of the village. Instead of seeing it, as Duvignaud does, as a moment when "society comes out of itself, escapes from its own definition,"[13] we will regard it as an occasion when society goes into its deepest self, that part that normally escapes it, in order to understand and restore itself. The cause of the distance between routine and *fiesta* lies in everyday history, in what they lack or do not understand at work, in their family life, and in their powerless dealings with death.

We can understand the difference of the *fiesta*, its excesses, waste, and widespread decorations, if we relate them to everyday needs. From a materialist approach, they can be interpreted as ideal or symbolic compensation for economic shortfalls. Behind the wantonness and sublimation of the *fiesta*, a dynamic (psychoanalytic) interpretation reveals the outburst or hidden realization of desires repressed in social life. In both instances, discontinuity represents one manner of talking about what is left behind, another way to keep it going. I do not agree that the essence of the *fiesta* is escape from the social order, the pursuit of a place "without structure or codes, the world of nature where only the forces of the 'it' are at work, the great instances of subversion."[14] On the contrary, it is through the ritual of the *fiesta* that the village imposes a certain order over powers it feels are beyond control; it seeks to transcend the coercion or frustration of limiting structures through their ceremonial reorganization, and it visualizes alternative social practices, which sometimes are enforced during the permissive period of celebration. These practices are not always liberating (they might be evasive when misfortune is construed in a resigned or guilty fashion), but they are structured, both by their own internal order and by the confined space they take up in the routine that comes before and after them and defines them.

The *fiesta* prolongs daily existence to such an extent that its development reproduces society's contradictions. It cannot become a place for subversion or egalitarian free expression, or if it does it is with reluctance, because it is not just a movement of collective unification; it duplicates social and economic differences. Thus, I do not share the view that recreational and monetary expenditure for the *fiesta* is a mechanism of economic redistribution or leveling: communal pressure for wealthy members to take up *cargos* and *mayordomías* is regarded by authors like Castile as a means to force them to reinvest their profits on celebrations, thus reducing income inequality.[15] I have occasionally found this process of coercion at work, and I believe it is legitimate to regard it as one way of making sure that the surplus is reinvested within the village, thus preventing greater exchange with the outside world from destroying internal cohesion. However, apart from the fact that there is no redistribution because wealthy individuals do not transfer part of the profits to the poor but spend them instead on the celebrations, this "loss" is often compensated by other earnings: they are also the ones who sell beer and food, who run the entertainment. By benefiting those who are already better off and enabling them to earn even more through increased consumption, the *fiesta* reasserts social differences and offers another opportunity of internal and external exploitation of the village. While it includes elements of collective solidarity, the *fiesta* displays those inequalities and differences that stop us from idealizing Indian "communities" and make us use this term with certain reservation when it is applied to such villages. (We cannot speak of communities as if they constituted homogeneous blocks; the term can be used to refer to groupings where collective factors are stronger than in "modern" societies, as long as we point out their internal contradictions.)

Having considered the fiesta as a *structure,* homologous or opposite to the social structure, we can now understand those elements in it that represent occurrence, transgression, and reinvention of everyday life and those that transcend social control and awaken desire. But tension between structure and occurrence does not manifest itself equally in every class and situation, hence the significance of first knowing both social structures and the structure of the *fiesta,* instead of speculating on the *fiesta* in general, and distinguishing between civic, religious, familial, rural, and urban ones. I will try to justify this theoretical approach with at look at three religious *fiestas* in Michoacán, namely, those of Saint Peter and Saint Paul in Ocumicho, of Christ the King in Patamban, and of the dead in the area around Lake Pátzcuaro.

Changing Popular Cultures: The Tarascan Case

Tarascans or *purépechas* have been and are still one of the major ethnic enclaves in Mexico. When the Spaniards arrived, they occupied the present-day state of Michoacán and parts of Guerrero, Guanajuato, and Querétaro, a total area of 27.6 thousand square miles, home to a million and a half people. This number included other ethnic groups, primarily Nahuatls, Toltecs, and *chichimecas*, but Tarascans constituted the dominant group. The few documents that tell about their pre-Columbian life, the *Relaciones de Michoacán y Tancítaro*, in which Sahagún echoes the respect Aztecs felt for them, are sufficient to give us an idea of their customs and power, their artisanal skills and luxury items, and their importance before the Conquest.

Colonized by the Spaniards, they lost land and independence and had to give up their customs to some degree, though many withdrew to the *sierra*. Through their stubborn resistance and the social action of Vasco de Quiroga, who took part in the process of colonization but became interested in developing certain Indian institutions, the Tarascan heritage was able to survive better than in other areas of Mexico. The overexploitation of the colony, fighting during the period of Independence and the Revolution, struggles between *agraristas* and *sinarquistas*— which upset and changed their cultural continuity—did not entirely destroy communal experience in the exploitation of land and forests, local organizations of government, artisanal methods, and some rituals and *fiestas*. Since these changes in past centuries have been widely discussed in several works, particularly those by Carrasco and Van Zantwijk already cited, I will outline in chapter 4 only the most relevant background information necessary for the analysis of contemporary conflicts.

Arriving in Patamban by day: after traveling for an hour and a quarter on a dirt road, we can see semiarid plots of land, some cracked, and during the best months, a few fields of corn, beans, and squash. Despite the lack of rain, vast pine woods surround the village. The inhabitants seem used to the cold characteristic of an altitude of 12,000 feet, and they leave very early, men and youths, on horses and mules, carrying axes and saws, in search of wood and resin. Around the houses—most of them built from large logs, others made of adobe—women, children, and a few men look after animals, tend small plots, and make green earthenware with ornate designs, which is taken to the *plaza* or displayed at their door during *fiestas*. They also go to the *plaza*, along dirt or half-paved streets, to fetch water that sometimes is rationed and to buy what they do not get from their fields. The older people speak Tarascan, the young ones understand it, and the children learn only Spanish at school. Since the rate of migration is the same as that of demographic growth, their number has been stable at some six thousand for some time.

Arriving in Patamban on Saturday night, the eve of the *fiesta* of Christ the King: 1.8 miles before the actual village, we know we are near because the wheel of fortune, as high as the church tower and lit with neon lights, can be seen in the distance. Through uneven streets, unaccustomed to cars and trucks of state agencies and private traders who come to collect crafts from the competition, we keep close to houses to let vehicles by, and we listen to the remarks of villagers who turn the doors of their houses into theater seats. In the *plaza* and surrounding streets, the younger ones gather to watch how stalls with manufactured goods and arcade and chance games are set up. As in other peasant villages, we notice that one way of "dressing for the *fiesta*" is to wear T-shirts and jackets with designs of American sports teams, bought during their work stay on the other side of the border; kids prefer to wear television images, such as Charlie's Angels and Bionic Woman. On the platform above the fountain, a representative of the delegation from the Office of Tourism announces that the *pirekua* (old Tarascan songs) contest is about to start. The first group is ready to sing, and men (only men), some forty of them, approach them with tape recorders raised for the best position to record the music. After each song, there is applause and the sound of the "off" buttons. During a break in the show, they answer my questions by telling me that the recorders were bought in Morelia or in the Federal District, others in the United States, when they worked as *braceros*, and that they want to record the music to be able to listen to it when the *fiesta* is over and they have to leave again. The break is over and they go back to their places, next to the platform or kneeling down to form a circle, around a large loudspeaker: in their attitude of concentration vis-à-vis electronic gadgets, in their slow and careful motions as they move the controls, covered by their large *jorongos* (blankets) that protect them from the cold, we can see that the tape recorders are part of the *fiesta* ritual. Like so many ceremonial objects, they represent one way of appropriating and preserving symbols of their identity. It is apparent that what they use, where it comes from, and where they take it reveal how identity is changing.

The other area studied, that of Lake Pátzcuaro, particularly the town that bears that name, seems to indicate the direction in which the process is headed that we saw in its beginnings in Patamban and other *sierra* villages. Besides its better farming, cattle, and fishing resources, the lake region, due to its key role in the economy, politics, and culture of the region since pre-Hispanic times to the present day, also includes archaeological and colonial centers (churches, convents, cities untouched after four centuries), arts and crafts, and tourist services. An excellent road system makes it easy for Pátzcuaro's twenty-four thousand inhabitants to travel often and to get manufactured goods, magazines, *fotonovelas*, and newspapers. For these same reasons, the activities of many official agencies were also concentrated in this area: the Secretary of Human Settlements and Public Works, which builds, among others, workshops and stores to sell crafts; the Indigenista National Institute, which sets up schools and shelters and offers technical and commercial advice to farmers and artisans; and the Office of Tourism and its advertising campaigns. There is also an international agency, the Regional Center for Basic Education in Latin America (Centro Regional de Educación Fundamental para América Latina, CREFAL), until recently under the control of UNESCO: it devotes itself to communal organization and peasant education, and, in the decade of the sixties, it influenced artisanal production through studies, courses, technical assistance, and proposals submitted to governmental organizations.

However, differences among villages bordering on the lake—for example, two of equal political and religious importance since the Conquest, Ihuatzio and Tzintzuntzan—do not allow us to resort to evolutionary simplifications that would characterize this area as an example of what will happen in the *sierra*. Tzintzuntzan is a mestizo town that no longer speaks the Indian language and is economically and culturally integrated into the national society. Nearby, Ihuatzio—which is also only a short distance from Janitzio, opposite the island that is the biggest center of commercialization of the *fiesta* of the dead in Mexico—preserves Tarascan customs, language, and forms of social organization. This process cannot be conceived as a progressive and inevitable incorporation of traditional cultures into the capitalist system. It is more complex, with comings and goings, disconcerting coexistences, and multiple combinations.

I have not outlined all the theoretical and methodological bases necessary to pursue research within the historical and social framework of the region. I prefer to interweave data and remarks throughout the text, allowing the description of phenomena revealed during my fieldwork to be guided by a conceptual explanation, and comparing and contrasting time and time again the theoretical work against the empirical basis.

3. Artisanal Production as a Capitalist Necessity

Will arts and crafts remain a distinctive sector, with Indian methods of production and visual motifs, or will they disappear amid the systems of production and representation of industrial societies? It is common to regard arts and crafts as anachronistic objects. It is said that artisan workshops correspond to a different mode of production, that they have long been replaced in the metropolises by manufacture, later by factories, and that unfavorable competition with capitalist enterprises relegates artisans to carry out repair work or other marginal tasks for which manual creativity still proves useful. One can understand that "backward" forms of production should survive in Latin American countries, with their late and unequal "modernization"; however, how can one account for the fact that Mexico, which has experienced growing industrialization since the forties, has the highest number of artisans— six million—on the continent? Why does the state increase the number of organizations geared to promote a type of labor that accounts for 10 percent of the population but only 0.1 percent of the gross national product?[1]

We cannot explain the boom in arts and crafts hand in hand with industrial growth if we think of them as an atavistic survival of traditions or as dysfunctional obstacles to development. My hypothesis on this question is that arts and crafts—such as *fiestas* and other popular expressions—endure and grow because they fulfill certain functions within social reproduction and the division of labor that are necessary for capitalist expansion. In order to explain their survival, one has to consider which functions are fulfilled by arts and crafts, not in opposition to, but as part of, capitalist logic, within the present-day cycle of reproduction of economic and cultural capital in dependent countries. It is necessary to regard as a whole both material and symbolic aspects in the subordination of traditional communities to the hegemonic system and the way they complement, and interrelate with, each other. At the same time, we need to transcend the study of formal variations in objects and in changes in production, as is generally done, and take into account instead the entire cycle of capital: changes in production, circulation, and consumption.

Let us consider, first of all, why the traditional function of arts and crafts—to provide articles for self-consumption within Indian communities—changes. We can identify several factors, inherent in capitalist development, that have been responsible in Mexico for an increase in the number of artisans and a drop in their production for internal consumption in relation to the surplus available for external trading. Without seeking to offer a full count, we will look into four major areas where the causes for such a transformation can be found: the deficiencies in the agrarian structure, consumption needs, the incentive from tourism, and sponsorship by the state. In view of the fact that the relation of these elements to arts and crafts and popular culture has not yet been adequately studied, what follows is not so much a systematic conception as a hypothetical reformulation of this issue, a gathering of data, and a method to apply the latter in order to encourage future research.

"Solving" Rural Unemployment

Agriculture, the major source of income in peasant economies, is organized into very small units of production (*ejidos* and smallholdings), whose size does not make it possible to deploy the full labor force within the household throughout the entire agricultural cycle. Rudimentary technology, often pre-Hispanic or colonial, coupled with the poor quality of much of the land, is largely responsible for the fact that a subtantial share of agricultural production is available only for subsistence. The surplus is offered in the market under such conditions of exploitation that it never provides small peasants with a significant income.

Since the sixties, the chronic problems of the Mexican countryside have worsened. *Minifundios* have become increasingly less profitable, the price of many agricultural commodities has deteriorated in relation to that of manufactured goods, and, with rapid demographic growth, the land available is no longer sufficient to provide work for the whole peasant population. This impoverishment has pushed large numbers away from the countryside, encouraged the concentration of ownership of properties abandoned by *minifundistas*, and raised the levels of unemployment and thus exploitation and migrations: in 1960, 90 percent of private holdings in the central region of the country had fewer than 5.1 hectares (12.9 acres) each; in 1970, many of them were no longer in existence.[2]

In Michoacán, *ejido* lands represent a minority compared to those in private hands or rented on a temporary basis. Small producers, or those engaged in communal ventures, rarely get much more than corn, beans, and a few other products in quantities barely adequate for their families. If animals are raised at all, it is mostly for subsistence; wood from forests is used for crafts, dwellings, and fuel. Such limited resources force individuals to seek alternatives for survival: some make crafts, others work on other people's land (as day laborers, *medieros*, or sharecroppers), and those around Lake Pátzcuaro resort to fishing and trade with tourists. Many are forced to emigrate to the southern United States; some do not get beyond Mexico's northern states or big cities; others go to Apatzingán, within the state of Michoacán itself, where more fertile lands make it possible to grow melons and cotton for export. Many of the families interviewed, both in the vicinity of the lake and in the hills, have members who work far from their villages.

Given the impoverished and seasonal nature of agricultural production, crafts emerge as a suitable additional resource, and in some villages they become the major source of income. Without requiring large investments in raw materials, machines, or the training of a skilled labor force, they increase the earnings of rural families through the employment of women, children, and the men during periods of agricultural inactivity. They enable landless peasants to find an alternative form of subsistence. Artisanal traditions passed on since pre-Columbian times, their central role in many Indian cultures, have led some officials to believe that this type of production "will solve" the agrarian question. While the most basic knowledge of the rural question leads to disillusion with this kind of "patching up," the broadest study to date on employment and migration conditions in Michoacán—carried out by Anne Lise and René Pietri—shows that to this day crafts have served as the principal means to keep the peasant population in this region from migrating: the lowest migration figures correspond to artisans' children.[3]

From the peasants' point of view, artisanal production enables them to feed and keep their families together in the villages where they have always belonged. From the state's point of view, crafts represent an economic and ideological option to limit peasant migration and the constant flood into urban areas of a substantial labor force that could not be absorbed by industry and would aggravate already worrisome housing, sanitary, and educational deficiencies. A study carried out in 1980 by COPLAMAR (Coordinación General del Plan Nacional de Zonas Deprimidas y Grupos Marginados, or General Coordination of the National Plan for Depressed Areas and Marginal Groups) indicated the gravity of these problems: according to it, some three million individuals disguised their unemployment by taking up hawking—as shoe-shiners, trinket-sellers, "fire-eaters"—on the capital's street corners. The promotion of crafts, which provide work for producers in the countryside and for thousands of marginals in the urban marketing system, transforms "a situation of visible underemployment (a short employment season per year) into a situation of generalized invisible underemployment all year long through the juxtaposition or superposition of economic activities with abnormally low income."[4]

The Contradictory Needs of Consumption

The expansion of the capitalist market, its monopolistic and multinational reorganization, tends to integrate every country and every region within individual countries into a homogeneous system. This process "standardizes" tastes and replaces the pottery or clothing from each community with identical manufactured goods, their distinctive customs with those imposed by a centralized system, their beliefs and representations with the iconography of the mass media: the marketplace gives way to the supermarket, the Indian *fiesta* to the commercial show.

But, at the same time, the exigencies continually to regenerate economic demand cannot tolerate the stagnation of production at a level of monotonous reproduction of standardized objects. Changes in fashion and a redefinition of meaning in the advertising of products are deployed against the risks of entropy in consumption: we all wear jeans, but every year we have to have a different design; when we buy manufactured goods—a car, for example—advertising whispers secretly to us (all) that there are so many colors and optional extras to make our own different from the rest. Capitalism generates its own mechanisms for the social production of difference, but it also employs foreign elements. Crafts can contribute to this revitalization of consumption, since they introduce into industrial and urban seriality novel designs and a certain degree of variety and imperfection that offer the opportunity both to be different from the rest and to establish symbolic relations with simpler life-styles, a yearned-for nature, or the Indian artisans who represent that lost closeness.

Psychosocial factors and the connotative value of crafts are particularly important among foreign consumers. Gobi Stromberg, an American anthropologist who studied the silversmith's craft in Taxco, has recorded some of the motives that drive tourists to purchase crafts: to vouch for their trip abroad (and therefore the socioeconomic status and leisure time thus implied), for their "broad" taste, which is not locked up in its own context and is sufficiently "cultured" to embrace "even the most primitive," and for their rejection of a mechanized society and their ability to "escape" through the purchase of unique, handmade articles.[5]

There is, then, a twofold movement within the realm of consumption. On the one hand, Indian-made clothes and household items are worn and used less and less in peasant societies since they are being replaced by manufactured goods that are cheaper or more attractive because of their design and modern connotations. But the declining artisanal production is revived thanks to a growing demand for "exotic" objects in the country's cities and abroad. This apparently contradictory structure shows that, in the realm of taste, too, artisanal and industrial, "traditions" and "modernity," mutually entail one another.

Tourism or the Reconciliation of Backwardness with Beauty

> *While the area retains a charm of wild virginity, the town [Isla Mujeres] is not quite so primitive as not to offer the basic comforts to which the traveler is accustomed.*
> —Guía turística de la Asociación Mexicana
> Automovilística, p. 166

Nostalgic fascination with the rustic and the natural is one of the attractions cited most frequently by tourists. While the capitalist system proposes urban homogeneity and technological comfort as a vital model, as long as its basic project is to appropriate nature and subordinate all forms of production to the market economy, a multinational industry like tourism must preserve archaic communities as living museums. Here too it wavers between uniformity and the selective encouragement of differences. In a way, countries visited by tourists are one and the same: English is spoken in all of them, there is an international menu, it is possible to hire identical cars, to listen to the latest hits, and to pay with the American Express card. However, to persuade people to visit remote hotels, it is not enough to offer them a reaffirmation of their habits and the familiar surroundings to which they can quickly attune themselves; it is useful to preserve "primitive" ceremonies, exotic objects, and societies that deliver them cheaply.

Even more than an indigenous dimension, what tourists require is its blend with technological advance: the pyramids with *son et lumière*, popular culture turned into a show. This is easily confirmed in posters and leaflets printed by private companies and state organizations. An article in the magazine *Caminos del Aire*, published by Mexicana de Aviación and distributed through its agencies and through Boeing, promotes the purchase of crafts with such a twofold argument: they are made with "very ancient stone tools" and lacquered with vegetable thorns and dyes, but they incorporate technical improvements that guarantee a long-lasting product. "Some thirty years ago many earthenware artifacts were charmingly decorated, but they broke easily and were too porous for the modern kitchen. Today, earthenware goods are still beautifully hand-painted, but oven-proof."[6] The structure of this reasoning reveals two ideological processes: (1) to show that ancient and modern can coexist, that there is room for the primitive in present-day life; (2) to organize such a relationship, to bind both parts together (as it differentiates them, it subordinates the former to the latter, in the same way that the adversative formula "but" does: its repeated use to link artisanal and industrial really means that the former is fatally inferior and defective, that it can last when improved by that which is superior).

As if to endorse the argument that the paradise location mentioned in the magazine must be visited because of the way in which it overcame backwardness while preserving its beauty, the article points out that "the contemporary generation of artisans are studying in colleges or are already practising professionals. However, often the tradition of skilled and creative hands is so powerful that these *same* young people go back to their homes to work in their spare time with ceramic, carve wood or any other artistic activity."[7] The picturesque, the primitive, can seduce the tourist because of their contrast to his/her everyday life, but it is even better if the folkloric-advertising discourse can convince him/her that poverty need not be eradicated, that the "very ancient tools" can get along well with "the modern kitchen," that something "beautifully hand-painted" is no longer incompatible with proof of performance. The contradictions between academic and artisanal, between the professional world and the peasant world, can also be reconciled within the same individual, in the realm of subjectivity. How can this be achieved? The dormant traditions within us must be allowed to come out when we return to our homes, to help us realize ourselves ... in our "spare time."

The impact of tourism on the production of crafts (changes in quantity and design), circulation (the growth of intermediaries, fairs, markets, and shops), and consumption (changes in the taste of Tarascan society) can be clearly assessed in the case of Michoacán, one of the states with greater artisanal development and influx of visitors. Its strong pre- and particularly post-Columbian growth, resulting from numerous internal incentives (from Vasco de Quiroga to Lázaro Cárdenas), had never experienced such rapid development as in the last decades. Together with the other factors mentioned in the present chapter, the key role played by the inflow of tourists is clear. Statistics, still unreliable and incomplete, and interviews carried out by the author in markets, indicate that times and places of higher production and sales coincide with those of greater number of visitors: among the 2,071,439 tourists who came to Michoacán in 1977, more than 60 percent (1,264,035) went to cities with the highest level of artisanal commercialization (Morelia, Uruapan, and Pátzcuaro) in April and December, that is, for the *fiestas* and fairs of Easter and New Year's Eve.[8] There are no specific data for Michoacán on the total volume of sales, but a national estimate indicates that artisanal purchases account for 18 percent of the average spending of each individual tourist.[9] A particularly impressive fact was the invasion of the most famous place in Michoacán, the island of Janitzio, when, in 1979, its 3,000 residents were visited by some 70,000 tourists for the Night of the Dead (November 1–2). Even 250 craft stalls, among them regular stalls and some makeshift ones set up by natives and intermediaries from nearby villages, were not enough to meet the needs of the crowd.

In short: in tourist discourse and in the data, too, we observe the significant role that crafts and popular *fiestas* play in contemporary development. As an economic and recreational attraction, traditional popular culture serves the reproduction of capital and of the hegemonic culture. The latter accepts popular culture and needs it as an opponent that serves to strengthen it and to prove its "own superiority," as a place where one comes to get easy profits and the certainty that we deserve them because, when all is said and done, history culminates in us.

The State's Political and Ideological Action

The main ideological function of crafts is not fulfilled in relation to tourists, but to the residents of the country where they are made. This was already understood by the leaders who emerged from the Revolution of 1910, and who promoted artisanal and folkloric development in order to offer a set of symbols for a national identity. Besides measures of unification, both economic (agrarian reform, nationalizations, joint development of the internal market) and political (creation of a single party, of a central labor organization), a country fragmented by ethnic, linguistic, and political divisions needed the establishment of ideological homogeneity. The Hispanicization of the Indian population and the exaltation of its cultural capital in the form of a heritage common to all Mexicans were some of the chosen means. The new state and many prominent intellectuals and artists (Manuel Gamio, Othón de Mendizábal, Alfonso Caso, Diego Rivera, Siqueiros) argued that, in order to build "a powerful Fatherland and a coherent nationality," it was necessary to pursue a policy that included, in Gamio's words, the "fusion of races, convergence and fusion of cultural expressions, linguistic unification and economic equilibrium of social elements."[10] Salvador Novo stated in 1932 that *"petate* (grass) dolls, *jícaras* (drinking gourds), clay toys, polychromatic *sarapes"* offered Mexicans "an exalted racial sense and a consciousness of nationality previously lacking."[11]

The significance of what was then called "popular art" or "typical industries" was officially recognized for the first time in 1921; a crafts exhibition, formally opened by the president of Mexico, Alvaro Obregón, was held to celebrate the centenary of the Achievement of Independence. In the thirties, promotional exhibits traveled abroad. The Regional Museum of Popular Arts and Industries was created in Pátzcuaro in 1938, during the government of Lázaro Cárdenas, and the first *indigenista* congress, meeting in that city in 1940, approved a recommendation on "protecting Indian popular arts through national organizations." Since then, incentives have grown: specialist and socioeconomic studies sought to establish the problems involved in artisanal production and proposed new aid measures; funds were set up to provide credit, and regional and national organizations were created to promote production and marketing. The General Office for Popular Cultures and the National Fund for the Promotion of Arts and Crafts (FONART), set up in the sixties, have tried to coordinate those endeavors channeled through the propagation of official organizations—more than fifty throughout the country.

Victoria Novelo, author of the most complete study on artisanal institutions and policies, writes that, while the postrevolutionary exaltation of Indian symbols was preserved, the advance of capitalism made their meaning and function in later stages more complex. She distinguishes three periods following the initial impetus: (1) commercial exploitation of arts and crafts tied to the growth in foreign tourism and the concern to increase foreign reserves, which brought about their partial industrialization and a combination of Indian goods with those from other areas; (2) encouragement of artisanal exports aimed as part of a policy of import substitution to adjust the balance of trade; and (3) promotion of arts and crafts as part of a strategy to create employment and additional sources of income for rural families with a view toward reducing their migration to urban centers.[12]

One way or another, it is possible to see through state policies toward crafts what functions traditional popular cultures can fulfill in the process of contemporary economic development and in the reelaboration of hegemony. Capitalist expansion does not always need to destroy productive and cultural forces that do not contribute directly to its development if these forces hold together a large sector of society and if they still meet the needs of the latter and those of a balanced reproduction of the system.

Is Artisanal Production a Capitalist Necessity?

Crafts, therefore, both are and are not precapitalist. Their role as an additional source of income in the countryside, as contributors to the renewal of consumption, as tourist attraction and instrument of ideological cohesion, shows the variety of areas and functions for which they prove necessary to capitalism. However, we do not get a total picture of what is happening with crafts if we consider the situation that currently confronts them one-way, from the perspective of capitalism alone. Artisanal goods have also been, for many centuries, cultural and economic expressions of Indian groups. This double enrollment—historical (in a process that stems from pre-Columbian societies) and structural (in the contemporary logic of dependent capitalism)—gives rise to their hybrid nature. The analysis of this hybrid nature must travel a road between two precipices: the folkloristic temptation to see only the *ethnic* aspect and consider crafts as merely fading remnants of dying cultures; or, as a backlash, the danger of isolating an *economic* interpretation and studying them as one would any other item ruled by the logic of the market.

Indian cultures neither can exist with the autonomy supposed by certain anthropologists or folklorists, nor are they simple atypical appendages of an all-devouring capitalism. At times, economists who are most concerned with the material development of social formations have a theological conception of capitalism (they conceive it as God: omnipotent, omniscient, omnipresent), and they overestimate its hegemony to the point where they regard everything that happens as the mechanical effect of its macrostructural determinations.[13] In societies as complex as those under periphery capitalism with a strong Indian element, sociocultural processes are the product of conflict among many forces of diverse origin. One of them is the survival of communal forms of economic and cultural organization, or their remnants, whose interaction with the dominant system is far more complex than what those who talk solely of penetration and destruction of indigenous cultures imagine.

Many studies on popular cultures have started from this apocalyptic question: What can be done to stop capitalist modernization from destroying arts and crafts and other traditional expressions? Before searching for an answer, one must ask whether the question has been properly framed. It is necessary to rethink it from the perspective of a more complex notion of how the prevailing mode of production reproduces and renews its hegemony. The four factors set out in this chapter show that neither the state nor the dominant class is interested in abolishing artisanal production. No hegemonic class can wield its power and its ideology with total arbitrariness, solely from above downward; it needs the advance of the whole society, particularly in its historically progressive stages. Whether through technological and economic development that integrates all sectors, including their specific forms of material and cultural production, or because it must improve educational and consumption levels of subordinate classes in order to expand production and the market, the dominant project includes much more than the class that formulates it.

Likewise, we must take into account the particular role Indians give to their own products and the manner in which they bestow a new meaning and a new function upon those imposed on them. There is much more involved than the submission and passive mimicry often attributed to them. We will have a chance to assess this when we describe the meaning of crafts in the daily life of virtually self-sufficient economies, the Indian household and the peasant market, and when we compare it with the meaning they acquire in museums, supermarkets, and urban dwellings. The reason we have offered an *explanation* of their current function before a *description* of the facts, which came first chronologically, is a methodological one: the explanation must guide the description. We are not ignoring the fact that all explanations are formulated during the process of observation and description and that once an initial explanation has been set up, new observations may lead to its reformulation; but it is also true that observation without a theoretical framework is blind or illusory.

The contemporary meaning of crafts under capitalism would escape us if we were to consider them only from the perspective of their Indian roots. Those who begin from their ethnic origin are led by their own method to regard them as displaced remnants within industrial societies. Instead, an explanation concerned primarily with placing them within the logic of capitalist reproduction, where history is present but subordinated to structure, can comprehend current fluctuations and the boom and decline of different regions and periods; it can see them in terms of the division of labor and the different ways in which the subordination of noncapitalist forms of production to the dominant system is manifested.

It is clear that, in this process of relocation, artisanal products are no longer what they were during the period of precapitalist workshops; or in past centuries, as representative objects of ethnic groups; or in the early decades of the present century, as symbols of national identity. They continue to fulfill in part these functions, but new national projects changed their cultural and economic role, and in so doing they altered their role in social relations and in the definition of Mexican identity and of their own identity as objects. We must therefore find out what changes are taking place in the internal structure of Indian and *mestizo* villages and in the social meaning of crafts, and in what way the strategies of reproduction and transformation of capitalist modernization affect their production, circulation, and consumption.

Bilingual display of crafts.

Left: Shop windows at the FONART store. *Right*: Crafts with credit cards among the urban landscape.

Inside the store, crafts from different regions and ethnic groups are crowded together; their confusing distribution and the lack of labels indicating their place of origin conceal the objects' cultural meaning. All our attention centers on the aesthetic value of each object and its price.

The Saturday bazaar, indoors and on the plaza (Mexico City, San Angel).

Here and opposite: Crafts for urban consumption: next to antiques, copies of renaissance and colonial art, toys, and decorative objects.

Bargaining.

4. The Fractured Society

The history of domination of the Indians is the history of disintegration and dispersion. Since every society is a structured totality, each one of its parts has meaning in relation to the others and they mutually reinforce each other. Therefore, to attain its hegemony over ethnic groups, external domination has sought to break their unity and cohesion.

Early capitalist penetration into the New World, with the Conquest and the colony, broke up the Indian universe through the reorganization of pre-Columbian economic and cultural systems. With private appropriation of the land by the colonizers, particularly the church, communal ownership in many regions disappeared: while the imposition of the *hacienda* regime proceeded more slowly in the Tarascan area because the land was less suitable for large-scale cattle-raising and agriculture, by the nineteenth century growing privatization had succeeded in breaking up communal solidarity, intensifying socioeconomic inequality, and transferring a large part of the land and power to non-Indian landowners. A new ideological system, Christianity, was superimposed on the *purépecha* system, replacing it as far as it could, or absorbing and redefining it: churches were erected on top of pyramids, sacred places were given new meanings in a different cultural system, and pre-Hispanic dances, music, and theater were used to convey the Christian message.

Yet the Tarascans managed to preserve part of their communal lands and traditional forms of agricultural and artisanal labor. In many villages, woodlands remain collective property and land use is still decided jointly; in some, self-sufficiency is still more important than production for the market. Certain communities, especially in the *sierra*, still speak the Tarascan language, celebrate their ancient *fiestas*, and preserve forms of social organization and authority—government by elders, *cargo* systems—alongside the national regime.

What happened to crafts during this process? They had had a major role in the economy of many Mexican peoples and therefore in the shaping of their identity since before the Conquest. We know from the *Relación de Michoacán* that the Tarascan empire had organized a complex technical division of artisanal labor (well before the arrival of Vasco de Quiroga, to whom it is often attributed): hides were worked in Nahuatzen, cotton in villages in the *sierra*, those around the lake made reed mats, and Tzintzuntzan had pottery. Commercial exchange, with crafts being bartered alongside fruits and vegetables, was very intense; the size and activity of markets made a strong impression on Spaniards: the one in Tzintzuntzan, when lit by torches at night, was compared by one European traveler to the sight of a burning Troy.[1] The colonizers increased the variety and quantity of production, especially during the time of Don Vasco, who introduced European methods and taught artisanal skills to villages that had not known them before. Nevertheless, Indian designs, the iconography derived from a pre-Hispanic vision of the world, endured in textiles and pottery and survive to a large extent to this day. It would seem that, unlike architecture and music[2] and political power and kinship, which were reorganized under colonial and Catholic influence, crafts were better able to safeguard the ancient identity that vanished in other areas of social life. However, what four centuries of colony could not achieve was attained by the contemporary development of capitalism. Industrialization, tourism, and the mass media appear to be more effective in making potters from Santa Fe de la Laguna manufacture clay cigarette cases, decorated with reproductions of international labels—instead of pans used for centuries—and those from Ocumicho fashion their devillike figures piloting airplanes; they have also influenced designs of trays from Charula (where the best pottery in Michoacán is made, and a village that has most stubbornly upheld its own designs), which in recent times have increasingly depicted giraffes, an animal that has, thus, suddenly become typical of the central mountains of Mexico.

Recent forms of economic and political subordination of ethnic groups to monopoly and multinational capital have required the restructuring of traditional societies and their popular cultures. The current conformation of capitalist hegemony reveals more clearly something that can also be established for the colony: neither military subjection nor unequal economic competition are sufficient, not even—as it has been more subtly argued since Gramsci—if consensus is added to violence and exploitation. These three means are also used in the domination of Indians, but they are only *adequate* to assure social reproduction and control within homogeneously constituted societies. In multiethnic countries, the conformation of hegemony not only is based on class differentiation, it also rests on the manipulation of cultural fragmentation and in the generation of further divisions: between the economic and the symbolic, between production, circulation, and consumption, and between individuals and their immediate communal setting. Such fissures are present in homogeneous national societies, but they are far clearer and more decisive in societies that, like Mexico, comprise more than fifty ethnic groups.

Ruptures between the Economic and the Symbolic

We are encountering a somewhat vague phenomenon for those of us who live in large cities, where a marked technical and social division of labor sharply differentiates economic from cultural functions. Large urban centers emphasize this separation by allocating structural and superstructural activities to separate spaces: there are administrative districts, industrial zones, college campuses, business areas, and so forth. The relative autonomy between areas lends each one different dynamics: an ideological crisis or the entire resignation of the government does not affect production (at least not immediately), nor do economic recessions necessarily lead to political realignments or changes in social consciousness. Strictly speaking, none of these parts operates entirely independently. Industrial activity can grow under its own relative logic, but it cannot do so in just any direction; it will be in the direction made possible by the other elements of the social system: the availability of professional and expert personnel, the administrative apparatus, educational structures, and consumption habits. But it is true that capitalism has granted each area of social life a greater degree of independence than other modes of production and that it presents them as even more disconnected than they really are. Such isolation generated, among other things, the compartmentalization of scientific knowledge and isolated academic and theoretical structures, as if a single object of study—society—could be conceived in economic slices on the one hand, sociological parts on the other, or linguistic, psychological, and so on, on yet another.

Research on archaic societies has contributed, on the other hand, to a clearer perception of a principle also applicable to capitalism: the interdependence between the material and the symbolic. When one arrives at the *plaza* in small Indian peasant villages and discovers that the *jefatura de tenencia* (village hall), the register office, and the Conasupo supplies store share the same building, and that the *jefe de tenencia* (mayor in a peasant village) receives us at a desk surrounded by wheat and corn sacks, we begin to understand the way in which political government, administrative power, and economic activity are mixed together. The same unity and interpenetration of functions is seen within the family, a basic unit of agrarian production, artisanal work-shop, and educational and ideological apparatuses all in one.

In noncapitalist societies, and in many with Indian roots integrated into the capitalist system, where traditional forms of life survive, structure and superstructure are less easily differentiated than in ours. Economic relations are not circumscribed to spaces explicitly set out for them—markets, shops—nor are cultural activities confined within specialized institutions (rarely are they found in the kind of isolation similar to that of art museums or college campuses). Economic and symbolic factors are interwoven in all social relations and spread through all aspects of communal life.

Certain historians and anthropologists believe, therefore, that it is possible to refute the distinction between structure and superstructure, and the determination of the former over the latter. Radcliffe Brown has argued that the explanation and origin of the actions of Australian aborigines are found in kinship relations. Luis Dumont specifies India as an example of how religion and the caste system may be determinant in the last instance. I, like Godelier, believe that, on the contrary, these cases serve to confirm that material and ideal factors form an inseparable totality and that the former do not always appear at first glance to have the dominant role that capitalism has accustomed us to recognize; but they do not succeed in negating the economic as determinant in the last instance, since in every one of them the dominant superstructure functions at the same time as a relation of production. Kinship regulates filiation and marriage in all societies, but it is dominant among the Australian aborigines. Religion always organizes relations between men and women and the supernatural, but in India particularly it controls the entirety of social life. Therefore, it is not the special functions of kinship and religion (regulation of marriage and filiation in the one case, of invisible powers in the other) that turns them into dominant superstruc-tures; they fulfill that role in certain societies where, apart from their general and explicit function, kinship or religion assumes responsibility for structuring relations of production. This is what assigns their ideas, institutions, and those individuals who preside over them a dominant role in the social process.[3]

Just as kinship relations control land and organize labor in many hunting-gathering societies, there are societies in Latin America where it would seem that economic relations do not determine cultural production. A first glance at Indian groups suggests that the character-istic features of crafts (their style, their iconography) depend on ethnic or kinship structures. Would the hypothesis that relations of production and class membership determine the nature of cultural representations founder at this point? The answer, as we shall see, is negative. What must be made clear is that when kinship relations and ethnic groupings function as organizers of relations of production, when crafts are produced by them, the distinction between structure and superstructure—as Godelier states in relation to hunters—"is not a distinction between institutions but *a distinction of functions within the same institution*."[4] Only in more complex forms of production (those of industrial capitalism), or when crafts adapt to the rules of industrial capitalism (substituting the family as unit of production for the workshop with wage laborers), does this distinction of functions involve at the same time a distinction of institutions: the material production of earthenware is carried out in the workshop, its design in a studio, its administration in offices. This technical division of labor goes alongside the much more blatant social differentiation between those who provide manual labor and intellectual labor and those who contribute capital and appropriate the product.

In this last case, the proletarianization of artisans is clear because it manifests itself in the labor process itself. But one must also realize how relatively similar is the condition of artisans who work entirely within the household unit, as long as part of the labor, carried out according to pre-Columbian labor and symbolic standards, eventually becomes absorbed into the capitalist market. They are not, strictly speaking, proletarians because they retain ownership of the means of production, but their dependence on commercial capital puts them in a situation very close to that of the proletarian. If we do not take this dependence into account, but consider only the process of production within the community or regard the cultural aspect in isolation, we fall into the distortion of conservative folkorists for whom the artisanal problematic is limited to the preservation of the forms, methods, and social organization in which ethnic identity is rooted.

However, it is also difficult to perceive the peculiarity of this condition when only the *economic* dimension is studied or when crafts are reduced to their commercial circulation. This is the case with two different positions that concur in reducing the artisanal question to a technical and economic problem: the technocratic interpretation and the vulgar Marxist one. Technocrats, interested solely in improving product quality and establishing the optimum labor process, substitute, for example, wood-fired ovens for gas ones, which no one then wants to use because the crucial factor about such a change for Indian artisans does not lie in the technical procedure but in the move from the domestic unit of production (each household has its own wood-fired oven) to the cooperative workshop. At the root of the failure of artisanal policies conceived purely in terms of technical modernization lies a lack of global, economic, social, and cultural vision. Something similar happens when it is assumed that Indians will gain consciousness of their condition of exploited proletarians without paying attention to ethnic oppression, which, being more "concrete," is more obvious to them: however much the basic form of oppression may stand out when economic exploitation is singled out, such denunciation, detached from ethnic mediations, remains "abstract" and foreign to their everyday life. Political discourse that centers on concrete conditions of exploitation thus seems as alien as religious proselytism that proclaims itself solely as spiritual action. However, the spiritualism of evangelists does not prevent many of them from realizing that the messages that penetrate Indian communities are those that provide (Western) answers to economic *and* symbolic needs (biblical indoctrination in conjunction with a school or clinic and, above all, a new ethics that will help them function during the uncertain transition they are undergoing as they move on to an alternative form of subjection to capital).

Peasant villages with Indian roots that have been part of a process of integration into a national society since the latter came into existence preserve a certain degree of communal experience sustained by economic and symbolic structures: forms of production and life habits in which the family constitutes the key unit, a set of appropriate beliefs and material practices, a specific relation with nature, and a particular language with which to designate it. Hence the need to regard together—and much more interwoven than in "modern" societies—material and ideal aspects, class determinations as well as those of certain formations that cut across classes (what Cirese calls *transclasistas*, or cutting across class boundaries), groupings of natural (race, age, sex) or social (language, ethnic group) origins, which do not negate the existence of classes but pinpoint other conditions in relation to which class conflicts adopt special forms.

What are the consequences of the closer unity between the economic and the symbolic for the study of traditional popular cultures? What changes have to be made to our research strategy in order to take into account such unity, even though it is being eroded by subordination to capitalism? On the one hand, when studying the transformations of Indian cultures, we cannot limit ourselves only to ideal structures (design, the meaning of crafts), or to considering the economic base as an occasional reference point or including it by way of a setting in an introductory chapter. The combined study of economic and cultural factors, required in any research, is all the more necessary if one is trying to understand the process through which communities where both aspects are more closely entwined become integrated.

Such vindication of a combined study of structure and superstructure also has political significance. Capitalist modernization does away with the immediate existence of the unity between material and ideal elements, first of all, because it makes the process of production more complex and diversified, it divides the different human practices—cultural, political, economic—and it breaks a particular labor process down into various specialized stages. *Economic* and *political* concern to isolate in order to gain better control is superimposed on the need for a *technical* division of social life: artisans whose weaving sustains their own community have a good understanding of the relation between their work and selling and consumption, but when they sell their work to intermediaries (who take the textiles to an urban market or abroad to offer them in the end to unknown buyers) they lose, together with part of the value, the global conception of the process. Their loss is even greater if outside intervention causes a fissure within production itself by turning artisans into mere wage laborers (in a workshop or at home) who limit themselves to doing designs imposed by others and stylings of traditional Indian iconography that are not theirs. The separation between the material and ideal aspects of production appears, at the very moment of doing the work, as an extreme consequence of the dispossession inflicted by capitalism. The loss of economic ownership over the object goes together with the loss of its symbolic ownership. The distance that a capitalist organization of labor and the market establishes between artisans and crafts parallels the rupture between the economic and the symbolic, between material (commercial) and cultural (ethnic) meaning.

Fragmentation of the Social Process

This dissociation between economic and cultural can be better assessed when we examine it together with the displacement between production, circulation, and consumption. What happens to pots made by Indian communities according to the principles of manual production and the predominance of use value in virtually self-sufficient economies, later sold in urban markets and ultimately bought by foreign tourists for their aesthetic value and as decorations for their apartments? Are they still crafts? Debates around this question tend to become embroiled in the material continuity of the object, which seems the same as long as it is not perceived together with the social conditions that are changing its meaning. While *materially* it is the same object, *socially* and *culturally* it goes through three stages: in the first stage, there is a prevalence of use value within the community where it is made, as well as the cultural value that its design and iconography hold for that community; in the second stage, there is a prevalence of commercial exchange value; and, in the third stage, there is a prevalence of the cultural (aesthetic) value of tourists, who inscribe it within their symbolic system, which is different from—and at times opposed to—the Indian system.

The displacement of the social meaning of crafts, practically irrevocable each time capitalist development subordinates them to its logic, endorses the need to overcome the isolation of objects into which studies on popular culture tend to fall. Most Latin American bibliography has alternated between a romantic exaltation of crafts based on their beauty and a positivist or simply folkoristic ordering of individual pieces according to ethnic origin or formal structure. Rarely does it transcend classificatory erudition and description of objects, to place them within the process that created them. It ignores the fact that their value is not defined by substance or by intrinsic properties distinct from social relations. In fact, what happens is that whatever beauty or meaning crafts hold for Indians or for a researcher are attributed to them as though they were inherent qualities, but the partial role of these individuals in the social course of objects that is also determined by other agents—intermediaries, consumers, and the like—is not recognized.

This isolation of objects colludes, generally unconsciously, with the dissociation and concealment carried out by the economic system as it separates production from circulation and both from consumption. The restoration of crafts within the whole process, the analysis of their changes in meaning as they pass from producer to consumer, and their interaction with the culture of the "elites" are all ways of making them intelligible and finding anew a meaning that commercial power has taken away from us, from the artisan from whom it was grabbed to the buyer from whom it conceals an account of its origins.

Individuals Cut Off from the Community

When I asked the *jefe de tenencia* of Capula, a pottery-making village with 2,600 inhabitants, what his job was, he replied: "I am an artisan." And after a pause, he explained: "I am really a law student, but all my family and all the people in my village are potters. I also can work with clay, though it has been some time since I have done it, but I still consider myself an artisan." In contrast with an urban worker, who regards his calling as the result of a personal choice, influenced by job opportunities, a member of an Indian community that produces crafts believes that his work identity is determined from within the collectivity, that it derives from the global, cultural, and economic membership to the group, not from his personal location within the relations of production. Such dependence on the community does not weaken each individual member, as we might think from the perspective of our own individualistic habits. On the contrary, as Mariátegui wrote, Indians are never less free than when they are alone.

Practices by both private intermediaries and certain state organizations that promote crafts encourage the separation of individuals from the community. In the realm of economic relations, they select the best artisans, they deal with them on an individual basis, and urge them to compete with one another. In the political realm, they intensify preexisting conflicts between groups and leaders through the distribution of credit and the demand of exclusivity in personal loyalties. The disjunction between individual and society is also brought about as the bond between artisans and their products changes: design suggestions to make the work of each producer distinctive and increase its market price go to extremes, such as asking Ocumicho potters to emboss their name on the base of their devils. We were able to confirm how foreign individual appropriation of creations is to Indian cultural patterns when we saw in the house of the president of the solidarity group a set of over one hundred pieces awaiting the arrival of the FONART official, who was to take them away to be sold. I stopped before those of an excellent artisan, because I was drawn by her parodylike designs, a certain violent and irreverent play with colors and figures, such as that of a woman riding a motorcycle carrying a devil and a snake as passengers, or that of a cradle for twins that held devils looking both childlike and sarcastic. I soon learned to recognize her style, those constants that gave unity to her work and enable one to identify her pieces before reading her signature. But after glancing at some twelve or fifteen devils I came to one which was clearly hers and yet had a different name. I asked the president of the group, and he replied solemnly: "It's just that when she finished that devil she couldn't find her seal so she asked her neighbor for hers."

The use value and the sense of community that crafts hold for the village that both produces and uses them—predominantly practical as far as earthenware or textiles are concerned, symbolic in the figures of devils or ceremonial objects—are neutralized by the signature. Individualization confers an alternative value on the individual piece: it becomes unique or different, it removes it from the system of *huipiles* worn for warmth or of devils that evoke Tarascan myths, to relocate it within the system of an artisan's work. The value that stemmed from the usefulness of the object to the community comes to depend on the singular gesture of the producer. Thanks to the signature, the meaning of crafts— as Baudrillard observed in relation to works of art—is no longer comprehensible in terms of their bond with nature or social life but must instead be interpreted in relation to the creator's other works.[5] The consequence for the latter is clear: segregated from their community, the creators' world becomes their style. Since their works no longer inhabit their village, artisans can only live within the universe of stereotypes that the market has established around their signature. For the few who succeed commercially, the final step in this uprooting will be migration to the city: their products will no longer be considered crafts, to become, instead, "artistic"; their name will vanish from the community and will begin to be known by collectors and dealers. For most artisans, who never attain such "privileges," the deculturation of their works entails a double life: they carry on sharing life in the community from where their objects came, and at the same time they take them to shops and urban markets, where they are subject to the vicissitudes of a foreign meaning.

A signature, which among artists is something of a personal affirmation and narcissistic game, becomes to artisans a paradoxical endorsement of their alienated identity. Capitalist modernization turns them into individuals without a community, seekers of a solitary place in a system that evades them. Closer than the widespread displays of pain and squalor, there are chronic, everyday events whose discreet dramatic quality is as great. There is, for example, the eloquence of villages like Capula and Patamban, which, ranking among the best in Mexico for their pottery, still look like they did three hundred years ago—adobe and wooden houses, dusty streets—a solid testimony to the fact that their crafts, produced daily for centuries, hardly make it possible to accumulate capital. One has a similar feeling when interviewing artisans in a market and observing that they constantly try to turn any conversation to the subject of selling: the taut face or the evasive look of individuals who are trying to understand the "disconcerting" logic of questions about how they work and live in order to turn them into answers about how their goods are better. Even if there are no buyers whose time we might be taking and even if we make it clear that we are not going to buy anything, markets constitute the hardest places to carry out interviews. Artisans are not there to talk about what they know, but to find out how their work can appeal as a commodity based on a logic created by others.

Commercial Unification: From the Ethnic to the Typical

However, capitalism does not only destructure and isolate: it also reunifies and resets the scattered pieces into a new system: the globalization of culture. Temporary disintegration simply aims to create fissures where a controlling policy might be established. We recalled at the beginning of this chapter that, in order to function, every society needs a solid structure that articulates all its parts; the pluralism of bourgeois society cannot hide the fact that it is valid for a minority and that it is sustained by a centralizing, monopolistic strategy.

When one goes to artisan villages one finds, for example, pottery from Capula, lacquered objects from Pátzcuaro, mats from Ihuatzio. In the stores of Quiroga, a market city where the roads linking these three towns cross, pottery, lacquered objects, and mats become *crafts*. The hometowns are erased and shops talk simply of "crafts from Michoacán"; they are never described as Tarascan or Purepechan, names that—since they apply to the Indian group to which the three villages belong—would retain their ethnic origin when bringing them together. In stores in Acapulco, Mexico City, and large tourist centers, crafts from Michoacán are displayed in the same window as those from Guerrero, Oaxaca, and Yucatán, and they become "Mexican curios" or, at best, "Mexican crafts." Even in the state-promoted FONART stores, one can observe this dissolution of the ethnic into the national: signs and other advertising proclaim "Genuine Mexican popular art"; inside, pieces are often grouped according to what they are made of or what their shape is, and even when they are distributed according to place of origin, there are no signs identifying them or notices briefly relating the material and cultural origin of their production or the meaning they have for the community that made them.

In the Acapulco Center, a gigantic entertainment complex where the Mexican government built one of the largest centers to introduce the national culture to tourists, dances from Michoacán are shown together with those from Veracruz, *voladores* from Papantla, a cowboy from Jalisco, a *torito* with fireworks, a cockfight, and even manifestations of urban "folklore," such as *clavadistas* from Acapulco. There are no accounts of the precise origin of any of them, only vague references to the state from which they come. In any case, dancers and *voladores*, cowboy and *toritos*, all feature the colors of the Mexican flag either in their costumes or in the stage design. The need to homogenize and at the same time preserve the attraction of the exotic dilutes the specificity of each village or town, not into the common denominator of the ethnic and the Indian but into the (political) unity of the state—Michoacán, Veracruz—and each state into the political unity of the nation.

We have discussed dissolution of the ethnic into the national. Strictly speaking, it is a reduction of the ethnic to the typical, because national culture cannot be recognized as it really is by tourists if they are shown a compact, undifferentiatied whole and are not told how the groups that make it up live or about the conflicts with colonizers (and between ethnic groups themselves) that are at the basis of many dances and many artisanal designs. The unification under national colors and symbols, positive in a sense, as I shall argue in the concluding discussion, becomes distorting and depoliticizing when it leaves out the differences and contradictions that it includes in reality. Museums or shows that conceal hardships, history, and conflicts that produced an object or a dance promote disinformation as well as preservation, oblivion as well as remembrance. The identity they extol is denied when its *explanation* tapers into its *exhibition*. The greatness of the people whom they praise is diminished when crafts and ceremonies—whose value lies in the effort made to transpose to a symbolic realm, and at times to "resolve" imaginatively, dramatic relations in which nature made them feel powerless or oppressors made them feel humiliated—are enacted as spontaneous expressions, with that ease attributed to popular virtuosity or "genius."

The typical comes from the abolition of differences and the subordination of features peculiar to each community to a common *type*. It could be argued that tourists need such simplification of reality because they do not travel in the role of students. However, the commercial simplification of traditional cultures, as well as in the so-called popular press and television, almost always assumes that its audience has a lower intellectual IQ than it actually does and that tourism and entertainment are venues where no one wants to think. It seems to us a reasonable hypothesis for market research that the simplification enforced by the tourist industry is greater than that expected by the majority of consumers. Under the pretext of encouraging consumption, we become accustomed to perceiving reality through a dull mirror, with so few shades that in the end reality turns out to be less attractive than it might have been. Paradoxically, techniques of typification prove counterproductive for boosting the consumption they claim to promote.

However, since our main concern is not to provide incentives for tourism, I prefer to point out the consequences that this reduction of the ethnic to the typical has for political and cultural consciousness. If we consider that tourism, besides its recreational value, is one of the major vehicles to make us comprehend our sociocultural place within an increasingly interrelated world, the existence of a general policy intended to neglect the plurality of customs, beliefs, and representations is disturbing. If we consider that, in order to understand ourselves, it is useful to know that which is foreign, to see that others can live— sometimes better—with other customs and thoughts, we must infer that this strategy to conceal what is different is a way of blindly endorsing what we are and have. Tarascans, Mazatecs, and Mayas depicted as Indians, squalor exhibited as picturesque, and beliefs that correspond to an alternative relationship with nature, illness, or the future that are seen as superstitions are all mechanisms to hide the true condition of those peasants who supply us with cheap vegetables, fruit, and crafts. They also enable us to remain surrounded by privileges and prejudices without any outside challenges.

Three basic conditions of democracy, acknowledged since the rise of liberalism—recognition of a plurality of views and life-styles, learning to coexist with them, and exercising criticism and self-criticism—are proscribed if we are persuaded that the entire world is like ours, or is in the process of becoming so; when we travel to another country, we buy crafts in the same old supermarkets, and what could truly rouse our curiosity—different ways of making plates and cooking, of sewing clothes and dressing, of falling ill and resorting to plants unknown to us to get well—is hidden from us, under the laconic label of "Mexican (or Guatemaltecan or Brazilian) curios." By developing and systematizing our ignorance of what is different, commercial standardization trains us to live under totalitarian regimes, in the most literal sense in which they differ from those democratic: because they suppress plurality and submerge everything into a uniform totality.

The typical—that is to say, what tourism surrounds with harmless posters in order to conform it to our preconceptions—is like playing a trick on the reality we visit, but also on our own, on what might happen to us if, instead of going through a stage design, we were to immerse ourselves in those countries with a different reality.

I was in Quiroga one day interviewing a group of Canadian tourists when they asked me which, among the stacks of *sarapes*, wooden and plastic toys, ceramics from various regions, manufactured leather goods, and thousands more, were the "typical" crafts from that area. I first thought of suggesting they go to Capula or Ihuatzio, but I thought it would be pointless: tourist coaches with air conditioning and reclining seats do not change their route. I briefly explained to them that Quiroga was more like the department stores they would find in Acapulco or Cancún than a Tarascan village, and I began to visualize a plan to urbanize the Sonora desert and provide jobs for many of the unemployed. There would be a Great International Tourist Emporium, which would save tourists the weariness of having to travel so many hundreds of miles. Anyone who came to it would have the chance of boarding ships and planes that would simulate the appropriate motion and would be equipped with audios of multilingual conversations to grant verisimilitude to the intercontinental journeys. However, without having to board any vehicle whatsoever, they could visit various rooms, all nearby, where circular cinemascope projection systems with quadraphonic sound and smells would reproduce images and sensations from every region and every one of the fifty-six ethnic groups in Mexico. There would also be a selection of famous ruins, cities, and monuments from all over the world, reproduced life-size in acrylic. In the morning, one would watch a *peyotl* ceremony among the Huichols and visit Niagara Falls; in the afternoon, there would be Saint Peter's Basilica, an Indonesian market, and the pyramids of Teotihuacán; in the evening, we would attend a competition of crafts and dances from all the Latin American countries. There would be a guide service, whose itinerary from room to room would become part of the show for the other groups, as is the case everywhere else, and for an additional fee there would be guided tours by bilingual anthropologists or specialists from the various communities. In the corridors leading from one room to another, there would be machines from which, after depositing a coin, cassettes would play recordings of phrases spoken by priests during the Huichol ceremony and the Vatican mass, of the roar of the falls, and of vendors' cries in the market in Oaxaca as well as other endearing souvenirs. At a second stage, new countries and ethnic enclaves would be invented with the aid of a computer to entice visitors back for a second or third visit: there they would learn of new religions, of made-up plants to cure unknown diseases, of pre-Columbian arts, and crafts and dances that had been nonexistent prior to the moment when they were programmed.[6]

5. From the Market to the Boutique: When Crafts Migrate

We can examine changes in cultural identity by recording, as we did, the influence of external agents on traditional communities. The subject has also been studied in the processes of peasant migration and assimilation to urban environments. We are now going to consider it in the "migration" of goods from Indian cultures.

Crafts offer an exceptional vantage point from which to observe the speed and multiplicity of changes brought upon traditional cultures by capitalist modernization. Indeed, the semantic structure of objects is more malleable than that of people: an embroidered skirt for a village's patron saint's day can change its function and meaning within a few hours as it becomes a decoration in an urban dwelling, while the Indian woman who wore it in her village, having moved to that city, will keep alive for many years those beliefs that summoned her to the *fiesta*. However, compared to other rural goods removed from workers' control and ownership, crafts maintain a more complex relationship between their origin and their fate because they are both an economic and an aesthetic phenomenon, noncapitalist due to their handmade condition and designs but incorporated into the capitalist system as merchandise. Even after their "emigration" from Indian communities, they carry with them, in their blend of traditional and modern materials (ceramics and plastic, wool and acrylic), of representations (peasant and urban, Indian and Western), and of uses (practical and ornamental), the conflict and coexistence between social and symbolic systems. That is why the social course of crafts can be regarded as a phenomenon that is particularly helpful to understand the current vicissitudes of popular culture, the economic and ideological interactions between town and country, and the manner in which capitalist development redefines identity as it combines various forms of production and representation. Nevertheless, much as the social relations that created it echo in every object, we must look at the social and spatial relations along which it travels to account for the changing course followed by crafts. The subordination of traditional cultures to the capitalist system can, up to a point, be summed up by the different positions occupied by crafts throughout their journey. This is provided, however, that we pinpoint in what sense the organization of space *visually represents* changes in production, circulation, and consumption, class and ethnic conflicts, and relations between the countryside and the city. We will attempt to show that the reformulation of the position of crafts in diverse spaces enables us to trace the strategy of *decontextualization* and *restructuring of meaning* that the hegemonic culture carries out in relation to subordinate ones. It is not, therefore, only the incorporation of crafts into various contexts that represents the dislocated condition of their producers but also the loss of context, the exile from their native space—Indian life, the rural market—and their displacement to another scene: modern culture, the urban store, the museum, and the boutique.

Crafts in the Indian Household

We often listened to artisans tell how they make earthenware as we ate at their homes out of that very same earthenware, some of us sitting on chairs, others on planks. Next to one of the walls were stacks of clay pots for sale and, depending on the time of the year, different amounts of corn, in sacks or piled up by the adobe stove fed by firewood from the woods that surround the village. If there were no other rooms in the house, there would also be a few (bought) beds, or rush mats, made in villages near Lake Pátzcuaro, which were rolled up during the day to provide as much available space as possible. The table would tend to be to one side, such that the center of the room remained free, taken up only at night with a burner, around which the family gathered with neighbors, a visitor, or the occasional anthropologist.

But those men and women are almost always dressed in manufactured clothes. Even in those villages hidden in the *sierra*, a growing number of people cook on gas stoves with utensils bought in the cities when they go to sell their earthenware. Pottery piled up for home use or sale sits next to many manufactured goods; flowerpots and medicinal plants are not far from shelves where tin food and drinks lie next to chemically prepared medicines. The mixture of objects reveals a process of substitution of artisanal elements by industrial ones, of traditional methods of satisfying basic needs—cooking, healing—by other modern ones. In short, societies organized under a regime that until a few decades ago was virtually self-sufficient are now increasingly integrated into a system of commercial exchange. The presence of local pottery and some hand-made garments preserve the practice or the recollection of identity and a history whose validity depends, above all, on how important communal or *ejido* exploitation is for the village's subsistence. In villages such as Patamban and Ocumicho, where the crisis of the old model of agricultural production has reduced peasants to poverty or where inadequate rainfall has made the crisis worse, crafts emerge as an economic alternative that enables a large number of people to remain in the countryside. Thus, crafts assume a leading role in everyday life and help to reinforce cultural identity in a twofold way: because what is involved are objects, methods of production, and designs rooted in the community's history and because crafts make it possible for Indian families to remain together sharing communal life.

Crafts both belong and at the same time do not belong to Indians, they both find and at the same time fail to find a place within the household. It is true that they still form a system with the domestic unit of production, and thus underpin the almost posthumous life of that system. But they also acquire new meaning and new functions. Indians are aware that they produce more trays for sale than for their own or their neighbors' consumption, and they can observe daily that what they earn from them helps to further their precarious westernization: portable radios and television sets, clothes bought from urban shops, and objects and habits brought back by sons and daughters who went to the United States to work as laborers all gradually push crafts aside into a corner.

All objects take their meaning from the system of real objects among which they are located and from the desired repertoire of objects not possessed, but seen, described, and offered through the seduction of advertising. The material and symbolic subordination of peasant life to the capitalist regime, the insinuation of modern consumption through the mass media, tourism, and migrants' accounts reorganize private life—both the set of real objects that have filled Tarascan households for centuries and the symbolic cosmos of desired possessions, somebody else's, in relation to which the meaning of crafts changes. Even though peasants cannot buy most of what is displayed in supermarkets or what is advertised in the media, that world of goods and symbols enters the scheme of their reference points.

Fairs and Markets, Showcases of Peasant "Modernization"

Artisanal production, carried out within the domestic unit for subsistence and exchange with neighboring villages and identified with the economy and culture of the region finds its first and last locale in the Indian household: production and consumption take place within it. However, between creation and use lies the market. There are hardly any exclusively regional markets and fairs, where only goods from a small area are exchanged among producers, in stalls minded by them. Local markets become a pivotal point in the articulation of the peasant economy with the national and international capitalist system. This is confirmed by their two major functions: the extraction of surplus products from the region for distribution in the national society and the incorporation of the peasantry into the domestic market through the distribution of manufacured goods.[1]

Both the markets in the smallest Indian villages (such as Patamban, Ocumicho, and Ihuatzio) as well as those in middle-sized cities that centralize peasant trading (Pátzcuaro, Uruapan) carry manufactured goods, and even crafts from other states: merchants from Guadalajara and Mexico City, artisans from Guerrero, Jalisco, and Guanajuato, usually go to markets in Michoacán. These markets preserve in part the structure of old rural markets, with crafts displayed on top of rush mats on the floor together with vegetables, fruit, animals, and other products from the area, the sale and display of which is organized according to the needs of the local community. However, these markets—like Indian households—take in an increasing number of goods typical of the national society's system of consumption and prestige: plastic goods, transistor radios, manufactured ornaments. Direct commercial, social, and recreational relations between producers and consumers give way to others, characteristic of advanced capitalism, where intermediaries and sometimes large enterprises play a key role. Consequently, the old visual and economic organization blends with the "modern": next to precarious stalls with food and crafts produced within the domestic unit, next to "folkloric" entertainment and competitions, we find stands with refreshments, arcade games, trucks from businesses with headquarters in the large cities, and advertisements for the most popular national and multinational brands.

Despite the growing penetration of big commercial capital, its unequal competition with local producers, and the medley of goods of different origin and manufacture, these markets still make it possible to relate to the cultural sources of certain objects. In small peasant and artisan stalls, the salesperson is almost invariably the producer, and the family organization that created the crafts displayed is present in the stall: the man, woman, and children who produced the various articles are the same individuals who advertise and sell them. We can witness not just a commercial fact but the entire life of the family, since they eat, sleep, and have household items and fragments of their daily life in the stall. "A dramatic and temporary museum of everyday life" is how Malinowski and De la Fuente described the market in their study of those in Oaxaca.[2]

Unlike urban crafts shops, which establish a distance between crafts and life and mix various cultures indiscriminately, crafts in a market get their meaning from their proximity to other peasant products from the same region and to the producers. The contrast is even greater in supermarkets, those anonymous and sumptuous storehouses where commercial abstraction reaches the height of ostentation: in the concealment of the owner—unknown even to the sales personnel—the technical division of labor and the reduction of the worker to his/her role (salesperson, supervisor, security guard), and the closed and aseptic organization of space, artificially lit day and night. A popular market, on the other hand, operates in open and noisy surroundings, often in *plazas*; it encourages changing interpersonal relations and usually holds traffic up or blends with it. Far from being confined to the formal relations involved in the commercial transaction, communication in the market embraces family life, politics, and health (let us remember that stalls where herbs are sold are also consultation centers). Even simple commercial exchange incorporates that keen and picaresque form of dialogue, namely, bargaining. As J. Martín Barbero has remarked, whereas in the supermarket relations of individual appropriation of objects are carried out in a quiet and solitary fashion—one can buy "without abandoning the specular narcissism which guides one from article to article"—in the market, people shout, we look for expansive communication, and allow others to address us.

In the supermarket there is no communication, there is only information. There are not even salespersons, strictly speaking, but only people who pass on any information which the package or advertising did not offer. Subjects in a supermarket do not have the remotest possibility of speaking on their own initiative without breaking the magic of the atmosphere and its functional character. Raise your voice and you will find yourself surrounded by strange looks and rejection . . . In the *plaza*, on the contrary, seller and buyer are exposed to one another and to everybody else. And in that way communication cannot be reduced to a mere anonymous one-way transfer of information.[3]

Nevertheless, the popular market increasingly resembles a supermarket, adopting its habits and allowing infiltration and restructuring. Just as Bourdieu argues that the supermarket is the art gallery of the poor,[4] it is possible to see in the rearrangement by tourism of the peasant market the simultaneous creation of two illusions: for the Indian, the "opportunity" to consent to the urban consumer whirl; for the tourist, that of believing that the encounter with traditional culture in its source can take place under the same codes that govern commercial relations in the city.

But there might be another illusion, that of the researcher or the reader who might be carried away by this opposition and would in Manichean fashion identify the peasant market with good and the supermarket with evil. Exploitation is also found in rural fairs and markets: middlemen who double prices, officials who speculate on the two or three yards of *plaza* to be taken up by each stall, artisans who sell a set of seventy-two dishes (the labor of a family of seven for fifteen days) for half the monthly minimum wage. We have already said, furthermore, that if artisans submit to such exploitation it is because back in their home village, working the land, they suffer a greater one. Capitalist relations realized in the supermarket and purchasing privileges manifested in the city and through tourism are sustained by the exploitation of the peasantry and the urban proletariat.

Crafts in the City: Instructions for Their Disuse

Take six million artisans, put them to work producing skirts and pans, necklaces and masks, like the ones they make for themselves but increasing their numbers by a hundred or a thousand; organize markets and fairs in small towns and set up curio shops in every tourist center. Then, one has to talk to merchants of every region, particularly if they have trucks to collect the work of artisans reluctant to travel and convince them that by acting as intermediaries for these goods they will earn more than with any other product. Last, one must run advertising campaigns on the beauty of the region, with leaflets that talk of the spiritual-folkloric-indigenous value of crafts, and place posters in every world metropolis and airport to remind people of the importance of finding nature and to point out that where crafts are sold there are also lakes, waterfalls, regional cuisine, and ruins of non-Western cultures; then one must invite millions of tourists to bring their urban weariness, their cameras, and their credit cards.

Surplus production of crafts, created in part by increase in demand (tourism, new consumer patterns, state promotion) in turn generates spaces and mechanisms that expand their rural commercialization. Artisans also go to urban markets, fairs outside their region, hotels and shops. But it is not easy for them to stay in a city for several days given the expenses and sacrifices incurred. In Michoacán, there are three fairs that rate among the best attended in the country: one in Uruapan during Holy Week, and two in Pátzcuaro—one the first week of November in connection with the Day of the Dead and the other December 5–9 (until three years ago, the latter was called the Annual Agricultural and Crafts Fair; now it has become the Tourism and Crafts Fair). At all three, there is a daily fee of one hundred to two hundred pesos for every square yard taken, and artisans sleep there every night, on the surface of the *plaza*: it is not metaphorical to say that popular culture is at the mercy of the elements.

They fare even worse in big cities, where lodging and food soon exceed gains obtained from the sale of their products. Furthermore, most artisans feel bewildered and insecure in such a vast and different world. To whom should they sell? Will they be swindled? Will the money earned compensate for days away from work, for individual pieces that break frequently because they are so fragile, and for the expenses incurred, which are much higher than at home? Because of all this, many artisans sell to private intermediaries (local profiteers and foreign traders) or to state agencies. While the latter's profits are smaller, I never came across an instance when there was less than an 80 percent difference between the money handed over to the producer and the price offered to consumers; generally, the sales price is double what the intermediary pays. But the majority of artisans would rather give up half their profit than run risks that they feel are beyond their control.

This expansion of the market is one of the main factors that have transformed the structure of production, the social position, and the meaning of crafts. In the realm of *production*, the era when most articles were made for subsistence has come to an end; the labor process, raw materials, and the design and quantity of articles have been modified to make them suitable for external consumption. They have been removed from a social system in which production and exchange were regulated by communal, even ritual, organization, and have been relocated within a regime of intercultural competition that artisans understand only in part and that they serve from outside. As regards relations of production, these changes bring about progressive concentration and generalization of wage labor. In cases such as pottery, there is a transition from family workshop to small industry or unit of production based on wage labor; in the case of textiles or furniture, the trend is to increase the size of enterprises and reduce their number and to mechanize methods of production, retaining only the formal appearance of the original crafts.[5]

A great part of the decision-making power about what crafts should be like is transferred from the sphere of production to that of *circulation*, or, to be precise, to intermediaries—a growing sector of merchants, rarely artisans themselves, who nonetheless control production and who enrich themselves at a pace unusual for those who begin with such meager capital. If the merchant has a truck, and perhaps a storeroom in the village, his dealings with artisans, as Victoria Novelo remarked, are in the nature of a "cottage industry, where the entrepreneur—the owner of commercial capital—assigns work to potters, buys their work and also has them bound to him through loans and cash advances";[6] there is no need for him to invest in premises for production or equipment (artisans contribute their tools), and neither does he have to take care of breakages or losses or—of course—such details as social security. Those intermediaries who also own workshops hardly ever reinvest their gains in technical improvements, because the handmade and rudimentary nature of crafts is precisely an attraction for consumers. The general conditions of the capitalist system and the very problems that artisans face when they try to work their way into it and organize themselves soundly make them increasingly dependent on commercial capital. This regime leads to the decline of local markets or their "urbanization" or "supermarketization," that is to say, crafts stop being part of peasant culture to become "folkloric" appendages of the national and multinational capitalist system.

For these changes in production and circulation to take place, there must be corresponding changes in the sphere of *consumption*. The growth of artisanal production depends on a new kind of demand brought about by tourism's passion for the picturesque, by a nationalism more symbolic than effective, and by the need to renew production and offer variety and rusticity within industrial standardization. But crafts rarely fulfill in the urban environment their original functions among Indian cultures. Their disuse is, strictly speaking, the passage from a practical use to a decorative, symbolic, aesthetic, and folkloric use. It is a change in their primary meaning, whose diversification and complexity might be captured in an extensive discussion of urban spaces where crafts are exhibited and used. In the following pages, we will consider four of these spaces, which seem to us to be representative of the major processes of redefinition of the function of crafts: crafts shops, boutiques, museums, and urban households. However, I want to say first that this change in meaning that crafts undergo during the passage from a rural to an urban setting, from the Indian or peasant culture to the culture of the bourgeoisie and the middle sectors, is counteracted by a tendency to reorganize the sytem in order to reduce the lack of syncronization between both cultures. Hegemonic policy does not just give objects a new meaning as it changes their surroundings and class basis; as we have already seen, it also changes traditional communities and urban consumers in order to attune them to the global structure. The adjustment between offer and demand is the result neither of an imposition on consumption coming from the sphere of production nor of an adaptation of producers to consumer tastes, but a functional and structural homology that orchestrates all areas of a social formation. Instead of looking into the conscious intentions of producers or the cynical calculation of intermediaries, the explanation must be sought in the capacity of the system to restructure objective relations and their internalization by subjects, in such a way that every aspect of social life tends to be organized according to a similar logic or to convergent logics: oppositions between crafts and art, between rural and urban culture, between producers' and consumers' tastes, are homologous both between them and with those that regulate complementary links between social classes. "The consensus thus established objectively between classes of producers and classes of consumers is not realized in consumption but through this sort of sense of homology between goods and groups," as Bourdieu pointed out in his research on taste structures within French society.[7]

I want to add that the perpetuation of a hegemonic class depends on its capacity to renew this correlation, this equivalence and complementarity between social classes, between the national society and those ethnic enclaves and subcultures that form it, and between social relations and the availability of goods. Inversely, the power of the popular sectors to effect changes will depend on their capacity to subvert this order and to introduce—in both the spheres of production and consumption—demands that represent their true interests and are therefore dysfunctional and that intensify the system's contradictions and thwart its restoration.

The Crafts Shop

It is possible to distinguish four ways in which crafts can be used: in a *practical* way, as part of daily life (plates, clothes); in a *ceremonial* way, bound to religious or festive activities (masks, pottery adorned with sacred scenes); as a *status symbol*, which serves as a means of social distinction for sectors with high purchasing power (jewelry, carved furniture); and in an *aesthetic* or *decorative* way, meant to enhance, particularly dwellings (*amates* or trees, mobiles.)

The urban shop displays crafts in such a way that these four uses are reduced to a combination of the last two. The practical and ceremonial use are mostly ignored as articles are removed from their context—the household or the *fiesta*—and displayed by themselves, without any explanations that would enable someone to guess their primary meaning. That is why one is so often told in stores that tourists ask what the purpose is of individual items or where they come from. And—what is worse—frequently salespeople do not know the answer. When I questioned buyers, I noticed that, with the exception of plates, clothes, or clearly practical articles, crafts were bought primarily for their design, for their suitability to enhance a corner of the house, or as presents with a similar purpose in mind. Undoubtedly, this corresponds to preferences consumers already had before walking into the shop. However, if one compares this predominance of aesthetic use with the prevalence of practical meaning in markets, even among tourists, one has to conclude that there is a correspondence between consumers and the arrangement of objects in shops.

There are several kinds of urban crafts shops. Some offer crafts and antiques, thereby associating them with the old, with what is no longer used and is bought only as decoration. Other stores, also private, crowd together crafts from many regions inside the same showcase or shelf, imposing, as a result of visual distribution, a certain degree of confusion, or simple indifference, regarding the origin and function of individual articles: unification is achieved under such vacuous formulae as "Mexican curios," already analyzed above, and by the most external characteristic, which makes it possible to display linen embroidery next to one of acrylic material, earthernware pieces next to china ones. In state shops (FONART, regional *casas de artesanías*), there are only "genuine" crafts, as they assert, which have been selected for their aesthetic quality: the emphasis on the formal value of individual pieces works better to elicit admiration, but it does not contribute much information about them; except for sporadic attempts through roundtables or a few audiovisual aids, the policy of these institutions is ruled by commercial rather than cultural criteria.

Differences between crafts shops correspond to the need to adapt the selection and presentation of articles to diverse consumer groups: those with relatively sophisticated taste, those who "buy" status symbols, or those who just wish to take back "souvenirs." This diversification in types of shops is also the result of an increasingly more complex competition imposed by the expansion of the crafts market and the growth in tourism. As the production and marketing of crafts becomes mass-oriented, some shops expand their stock (bringing together articles from different regions and of different value), while others, which appeal to consumers interested in aesthetic meaning and social status, prefer "authentic" works, those that become "exclusive" works by their innovative qualities. The ramification of supply and demand gives rise to changes in the structure and design of objects: in one case, simplification or mass reproduction reduces costs (e.g., the crass and endless proliferation of Aztec calendars); in another, stylization and the search for originality, which will enable consumers with high purchasing power to distance themselves from "common" consumers (signed textiles and ceramics).

The contrast between stores that increase their profits by carrying a greater number of products and those that try to do so through formal innovation of design corresponds to the contrast between aesthetic styles of different classes. On the one hand, there is the taste developed by petit bourgeois and popular sectors, which reflects a fondness for the more immediate expressions of the exotic in its standardized versions. On the other, there is the taste of the bourgeois and cultured sectors of the petite bourgeoisie, which emphasizes, through its concern for authenticity, its acquaintance with origin, and, with its regard for formal innovations, an aptitude to appreciate works of art independently of their use, thus expressing its distant relationship to the pressing economic needs of everyday life. In the same way, such diversification of sociocultural functions of crafts reveals the variety of social levels and strategies in which they are used and the extent to which their circulation today surpasses the archaic meaning of Indian articles produced for self-sufficient communities with a practical or ceremonial purpose.

Between the Boutique and the Museum

A museum, too, removes crafts from their native context and emphasizes their aesthetic value, but it does not price them; it simply puts them on display to be looked at. As it enters those neutral salons, seemingly outside history, each craft is detached from its semantic and pragmatic references, and its meaning is fashioned from the relations that its form establishes with those of other articles in the internal syntax of the museum. The glass panes that protect them and the solemn pedestals on which they are exhibited further exalt their isolated condition as articles-to-be-looked-at.

In boutiques, more attention is paid to the presentation of crafts. There they are displayed to be seen, as in a museum, but, while the latter rules out their private appropriation, boutiques show and arrange them in order to encourage us to buy them. Their intervention is not confined to the selection of quality pieces and their display alongside tapestries, antique furniture, and luxury editions; they alter the finish of certain articles, their paint or polish, in order to confer on them the "dignity" of luxury or old age.

In a museum, we encounter cultural heritage and the history of humankind's struggles with nature and other people, but they are locked up in display cases; a boutique neutralizes that past, or emphasizes those elements in it that can be subordinated to beauty, so that it can coexist peacefully with our present (a product that hides the tragedies behind its creation seems best to divert our attention from contemporary ones). In a museum, crafts cannot be touched; a boutique offers something that is also to be looked at rather than used, something that shows that it belongs to the person who buys it but that bears the sense of remoteness characteristic of the decorative, as if it was not meant to be part of life.

And, if crafts do not belong either to the artisan from whom they are economically and symbolically taken away or to the consumer who is forced to give them an external and foreign use, to whom do they belong? To the merchants, of course, though it would be more precise to say that they belong to those who jointly manage our money and our dreams, those who exchange our reality for fetishes.

Virtually everything that is done today with crafts can be summed up by the boutique and the museum, wavering between commercialization and conservation. While some people sell crafts, taking half their value away from the producer, a few blocks away they are being preserved and exalted as though they were above all material value, only an eternal creation of the spirit. Crafts museums embody the good conscience of a system whose axis lies in the market.

But, how can a museum help us comprehend the meaning of objects, the relationships between a mask and a container, a shawl and a *fiesta*? There have been many attempts to go beyond simple collecting or the aesthetic exhibition of items. The best example known to us in Michoacán is the Museum of Popular Art in Pátzcuaro, where crafts related to particular activities, such as cooking, are arranged in surroundings that reproduce point by point the structure of a traditional Tarascan kitchen. However, the first thing one experiences when one enters it is not life in a kitchen but the passive, monotonous, untouchable arrangement of the objects in question. The tour guide emphasizes the fact that most of the containers and textiles were made in the nineteenth century, and, indeed, their delicately faded color and the stiff neatness of their display induce a distanced and reverent glance.

It is not a matter of introducing mannequins, photographs, or audio-visual aids, though sometimes these can be useful. We must accept the fact that museums are different from life. Their task is not to copy reality but to reconstruct its relations. Therefore, they cannot stop at the exhibition of single objects or of meticulously arranged rooms; they must introduce the *links* between objects and people, so that their meaning can be understood. Why show only containers and textiles, never an oven or a loom? Why not show them being used? And what if we also documented the relationship between work hours and prices? Cirese is correct when he asserts that the isolation of objects in museums is much greater than that required by the need to preserve them, because the entire institution is pervaded by an ideology of passivity. While the conservation of objects does not enable visitors to use them as they please, there are many that are not at risk, and it would be feasible to make reproductions of the more fragile ones in order to show their use as well as their form.[8] To the extent that museums make people forget that pans were meant for cooking, masks for celebration, and *sarapes* for warmth, they are places that fetishize objects, just like shops and boutiques.

Inside the Urban Household: The Aesthetics of Souvenirs

I am visualizing the inside of houses of the petite bourgeoisie, the accumulation and proliferation of objects with which it seeks to show its achievements and entrench its privacy: a house as a mini-museum, a place of conservation and exhibition. A blender, a record player, a television, imported china, everything has its own runner under or above it, everything is underwritten, as in a museum. There is a need to overprotect that which one had the good sense to obtain. In a corner, on some furniture or shelf, as a sign that those who inhabit such zealous private worlds also travel, lie objects that proclaim places visited: Acapulco, Las Vegas, Oaxaca.

Every time we read "Souvenir from Michoacán," we know that that article was made to be used anywhere but in Michoacán. That formula, supposedly meant to guarantee the authenticity of the object, is a sign of its lack of authenticity. Tarascans will never need to stamp the place of origin in any pan or jug they make for use among their peers. Tourists need the inscription: that particular pot will be placed with others bought elsewhere, the objects themselves are not as meaningful as the social status and the prestige of someone who has been to those places and bought them.

The inscription is contradicted by the very fact that it is written. The fact that it was necessary to engrave its origin implies that there is a danger of forgetting, or not knowing, where it came from. Most articles that carry such a formula of identification are neither bought from the producers nor chosen because an emotional, concerned, and understanding relationship has been established between a foreigner and the people who make them; they are bought in urban markets or stores, often in regions other than those where they were made. The extreme parody of this loss of context is found in crafts sold in airports. Since tourists cannot learn anything about artisans' living conditions, a memory or the nostalgia of an identity unknown by them must be invented for them.

Since it destroys the use value of crafts through an undifferentiated exchange of commodities or through the almost hollow symbolic value of "Indianness," capitalism must create imaginary identities, invent memories, and call attention to them in order to generate meanings that can fill the void left by those that are lost. Having forgotten the use of objects that are now good only to sell and to enhance, to be exhibited and to confer status, having neglected relations with nature and with the society that gave rise to peasant iconography, what meaning can we find in forms—flowers that invite rain, broken lines to simulate lightning—evoking that universe indirectly?

Hence exists the need for the discourse of advertising to set up new meanings, to work out an imaginary social setting, in which the depth of the past is called upon to confer depth on a domestic privacy stereotyped by manufactured goods. Hence is the need for crafts to include that combination of label of origin and working instructions and the need to overstate folkloric elements when referring to crafts: hyperbole is the favorite figure of speech of the rhetoric with which capitalist modernization appropriates the exotic. When "Indian" or "natural" objects are subjected to urban culture, their distinctive elements are overdone: Oaxacan *huipiles* must have more flowers and birds if made for export, and there are no dances as colorful or Papantla *voladores* as vertiginous as those shown at the Acapulco Center, just as—Rubert de Ventós stated—the gardens of the Hotel Princess are more tropical than the jungle (there are more coconut palms, more lianas, more parrots, and more of everything). Adapted to the rules of commercial display, Indian culture offers something "better" than its essence: a magnification, a heightened staging of its beauty. Capitalist modernization has taught us to see the culture of the people through a specular rearview mirror.

The depth of the past is called upon to confer depth on a domestic privacy stereotyped by manufactured goods: a handmade pot and a *sarape* are kept in an urban household not for their usefulness but for their decorative use; they are not expected to play a part in the *space* of domestic practice but in the *time* that gives meaning to personal and family life. Crafts, which were mostly created in Indian cultures because of their function, are incorporated into modern life for their *meaning*. What is their meaning? Precisely time, origin. Unlike functional objects, which exist only in the present and to be used—a glass to drink out of, a car to travel by—old objects or crafts tell us about the passing of time and about origins.

The taste for old objects and for crafts, Baudrillard wrote, usually goes with a passion for collecting: to own in order to withstand time and death. To appropriate the past, to bring it together, to arrange it and to put it forward for one's own and others' appreciation is to keep it alive, to fight against the transient elements of the past. At a time when objects deteriorate fast and are discarded, the presence of crafts represents a triumph over wear and tear, it shows the beauty of that which survives. That is why a handmade object, "the most beautiful of domestic animals . . . a sort of intermediary between beings and objects,"[9] is given that special setting, a *private* corner that manifests the *personal* relationship which its owner has with the past. Hence, it is important to the bourgeoisie not to have ordinary crafts, similar to those of others. Not only has the bourgeoisie appropriated nature and privatized it through technical dominance, not only does it appropriate the economic surplus through social exploitation, it also appropriates the past, the past of social groups that it oppresses, and puts it at the disposal of its need for status. That is why it transforms historical time into metaphysical time and turns objects into symbols, other people's daily utensils into trophies that—like paintings, wines, and antique furniture—vouch for the fact that their owner has a taste for the old and controls time and history. The way in which crafts are collected in the houses of the bourgeoisie and the petite bourgeoisie is the exact opposite of the relationship that we have not known how to, or have not wanted to, enter with artisans: if we can look at crafts properly, we will find an indictment in this contrast.

Toward a Popular Policy for the Use of Urban Space

Each context determines the way in which crafts will be looked at, the deciphering codes. Those codes that govern their production by peasants and their place in the market, next to vegetables and fruit, are very different from visual and semantic codes that guide the perception of crafts in museums or those used for interior decoration in homes, where the aesthetic meaning of forms is more autonomous. In recent years, the bibliography on the artisan question moved forward markedly when it recognized the influence of official agencies as well as intermediaries on changes in the process of production and in design.[10] However, we do not know of any study on crafts that allocates to spacial structures a function equivalent to that of ideological apparatuses. Nonetheless, like the family and the school, the differential placement of objects in one setting or another induces habits of perception and schemes of comprehension and incomprehension.

The organization of space and the change of context and meaning of popular objects is essential to the construction of the bourgeoisie's hegemony. The latter's interest in crafts is not simply economic and is not limited to reducing peasant misery and migrations or providing easy profits for intermediaries; it also seeks political effects: to reorganize the meaning of popular creations and of their institutions—household, market, *fiesta*—in order to subordinate them to modernity.

An integral account of popular cultures must examine the various spaces in which their products circulate and avoid compartmentalized approaches such as those held by scholars who focus only on the labor process or marketing. It is necessary to observe interpenetrations between different spheres and between objects and their logic, for example, the way in which the industrial world invades the privacy of the Indian household, and, conversely, why an urban commercial organization would be concerned to retrieve the archaic, to link the present to the past, as souvenirs in urban households seek to do. It is also necessary to look into the reason behind a certain "fuzziness" between rural and urban, between Indian and Western, and between cultures of different social classes, to perceive the homogenizing and monopolizing organization of capitalism at the root of all such interactions.

That is why we reject the evolutionist, linear idea that conceives of Indian and peasant culture as a preindustrial stage, whose inexorable destiny is to become increasingly similar to "modernity," and, eventually, to disappear. While there is a tendency in capitalist development to make things alike and to absorb earlier forms of material and cultural production, given the inability of industrial capitalism itself to provide work, culture, and health care for everyone and the resistance on the part of ethnic enclaves that guard their own identity, the subordination of traditional communities cannot be complete. The ambiguous strategy of the dominant classes toward subordinate cultures can be explained, then, by this twofold movement: a desire to impose their economic and cultural models on subordinate cultures and, at the same time, to appropriate that which they cannot destroy or bring under control, using alien forms of production and thought once their function has been redesigned such that their survival does not stand in contradiction to capitalist growth.

Finally, this enables us to catch a glimpse of the direction in which we must proceed to construct a counterhegemonic culture. It is not enough to "preserve" popular culture and prevent the loss of legends, crafts, and *fiestas*. Nor is it sufficient to promote their production through well-intentioned credit or to seize their best creations for display in reputable museums or lavishly illustrated books. Traditional myths and medicine, crafts and *fiestas*, can work toward the improvement of the quality of life of the popular sectors so long as they are acknowledged by the latter as identity symbols around which they can cohere, and so long as Indians and urban popular classes can manage to convert those "remnants" from the past into "emergent," challenging expressions.[11] To achieve this, it is fundamental that the popular sectors organize themselves into cooperatives and unions from which they can begin to regain ownership of the means of production and distribution. But it is also vital that they succeed in appropriating the symbolic meaning of their work. Obviously, this does not mean their reintegration into an Indian context or the "Indianization" of urban shops, but the formulation of a strategy for gradual control over spaces and mechanisms of circulation.

Such a strategy has to differentiate between those elements of popular cultures that constitute mere survival and those that represent the contemporary interests of the subordinate classes and can oppose the hegemonic system. It then needs to consider the opportunities available to producers in markets and fairs and to demand active participation in their organization and management, in tourist advertising, in the appointment of panels of judges in shows, and so on—in short, to fight for economic and cultural control over production and all instances in which its function and meaning can be reformulated. As regards innovations in design, presentation, and distribution of their products, it will be up to artisans, dancers, and Indian cultural workers to decide which changes should be endorsed and which ones clash with their own interests. A popular culture will emerge in proportion to the degree to which urban and rural popular classes play such a key role: a culture that will emerge democratically from the critical reconstruction of lived experience.

6. *Fiesta* and History:
To Celebrate, to Remember, to Sell

Rural *Fiestas* and Urban Shows

The *fiesta* can be regarded as a staging of fissures between the country-side and the city, between Indian and Western elements, their interactions and conflicts. This is demonstrated by the coexistence of ancient dances and rock groups, by hundreds of Indian offerings to the dead being photographed by hundreds of cameras, by the crossing of archaic and modern rituals in peasant villages, and by the hybrid *fiestas* with which migrants in industrial cities invoke a symbolic universe centered around corn, earth, and rain. Such dramatic oppositions are also represented in the contrast between rural and urban *fiestas*.

In Indian and peasant villages, *fiestas* constitute collective events firmly rooted in production, celebrations set according to the rhythm of the agricultural cycle or the religious calendar, where the domestic unity of life and work is reproduced in the joint participation of the family.

In cities, class divisions, other family relationships, the higher degree of technical and commercial development applied to leisure, and mass organization of social communication create a different kind of festivity. People attend most *fiestas* as individuals; the *fiestas* fall on arbitrary dates and, when they conform to the ecclesiastical calendar, their structure follows a commercial logic that turns the religious motivation into a pretext; instead of communal participation, they offer a display to be admired.

Gilberto Giménez gives an outline of some characteristics of rural and urban *fiestas* in the model on pages 88 and 89.[1] This type of comparison has given rise—as in the case of arts and crafts—to Byzantine controversies on what are the essential elements of the *fiesta*, on the exclusive authenticity of the rural *fiesta* and its decadence in urban variations.[2] As Giménez warns, this polarization is too "abrupt," and in fact it is difficult to find unadulterated communal *fiestas*, with impeccable Indianness. We will also explore to what extent a rupture of social time, the predominance of use value, and other features pointed out do in fact

Traditional Peasant Fiesta

(a) Break with regular time.

(b) Collective nature of the festive phenomenon, with no exclusions of any classes, as expression of a local community.

(c) Comprehensive and global nature through which the *fiesta* embraces the most heterogeneous and diverse elements without segregation or "specialization" (games, dances, rituals, music, etc., within one global celebration).

(d) Consequent need to spread out into large open spaces and outdoors (the *plaza*, the church atrium).

(e) Highly institutionalized, ritualized, and sacred nature (the traditional *fiesta* is inseparable from religion).

(f) Infusion of the *fiesta* with the logic of use value (from which: *fiesta*-participation, not *fiesta*-show).

(g) Strong reliance on the agricultural calendar within the framework of an agricultural system dependent on rainfall.

---

occur. The more relevant questions in our view are those that will help us understand why such a contrast exists, why rural *fiestas* increasingly yield to urban commercial patterns and are partially replaced by entertainment and shows.

We will study three *fiestas* in which, in the terms of functionalist evolutionism, one might observe a transition from rural to urban or from traditional to modern: the patron saint's *fiesta* in Ocumicho, celebrated year after year with no significant changes; that of Christ the King in Patamban, where the modifications I noticed throughout a period of three years represent the village's increasing adherence to the national market and urban culture; and, finally, the *fiesta* of the dead in the area around Lake Pátzcuaro, where I compared the traditional celebration in Ihuatzio and other villages with its radical variation, a few hundred yards away, on the island of Janitzio, as a result of the commercial reorganization of this festivity. However, we will not treat these three cases as stages in a progression—the *fiesta* in Ocumicho is not doomed to become like Janitzio's—but as processes that reveal changes unleashed by capitalist penetration in a cultural tradition, that is, the Tarascan. Furthermore, given their religious meaning, all three cases will lead us to examine the prevalence and lapse of traditional beliefs and their current role in the redefinition of popular cultures.

Urban Fiesta

(a) Integration of the *fiesta* into daily life as an appendage, complement, or compensation.

(b) Highly privatized, exclusive and selective nature of the *fiesta*.

(c) Its extreme differentiation, fragmentation, and "specialization"
(the elements that coexisted within the unity of one global celebration in the popular *fiesta* are separated).

(d) Consequent need to proceed in intimate and enclosed spaces.

(e) Laicization and secularization of the *fiesta*, greater spontaneity,
and less reliance on a stereotyped calendar.

(f) Penetration of the logic of exchange value: *fiesta*-show, conceived
from the point of view of consumption, not *fiesta* participation.

Because It Does Not Rain, the Saints Will March with Their Backs Turned

Pine woods surround the village. Its people make a living from wood and
resin, but also from the cultivation of very small plots, where corn and
beans grow as best they can during the few rainy months. Some villagers
breed lambs and sell the wool. Of the 2,300 residents of Ocumicho, 65
families make pottery and a few women weave blouses. Their way of life
is similar to our description of Patamban's. The first difference that
strikes an observer is the fact that everyone speaks Tarascan all day long;
young men and some women use Spanish when outsiders visit them.
Besides the language, they are held together by a strictly safeguarded
system of *compadrazgo* (compaternity) and communal solidarity: there
are some households where four and five families, who sow and harvest
the land jointly, live together.

Why, at the end of the 1960s, did they begin to make those clay
devillike figures that quickly became one of the most widespread and
valued Mexican crafts? The story goes: "The devil used to go through
Ocumicho, bothering everybody. He would go into trees and kill them.
He would get inside dogs and they would do nothing but shake and howl.
Then he pursued people and they would become ill or mad. Somebody
thought that he should be given places where he could live without
bothering anyone. That is why we made clay devils, so that he could have
somewhere to stay."

By putting this account together with two facts, a particular interpretation began to emerge. On the one hand, the time when devils were first

made coincided with a period when there was little rainfall, and *ejidatarios* from Tangancícuaro appropriated some very fertile lands, which Ocumicho residents have been unable to recover to this day. While a few had made pottery before, it now became an alternative activity for many families, the exploitation of woodlands was intensified, and trade with the national market increased. The second fact that can be linked to the myth is certain constants featured in the devils: they are surrounded by snakes and animals from the region, but they are normally associated with elements from the "modern" world not present in the village: policemen, motorcycles, airplanes. The largest ceramic we came across in Ocumicho, twenty-seven inches long, was a bus full of merry devils, hanging out of the windows, and the inscription in the front, Ocumicho-Mexico-Laredo (the village's name being part of a sequence together with two places to which migrants go in search of work). Might we not think that the devils—the lack of rainfall, the theft of lands, the need to open up the community to the outside world, all the wrongs that began to break them up—needed a place where they could be contained and controlled?

Fiestas fall between the few spaces where they can continue to reassert their communal solidarity. The four *barrios* that make up the village share the organization and financing of the main *fiestas*, which are Saint Sebastian on January 20, Lent during Holy Week, Saint Peter and Saint Paul on June 28 and 29, the Holy Christ on September 13 and 14, the Virgin on December 8, and then the Christmas *pastorelas* and Saint Stephen and Saint Michael on December 26 and 27. They appoint *cargueros* (holders of *cargos*), but everyone contributes money and labor. Nothing could be further from a show. The activities for each *fiesta* and the manner in which they are carried out are known to the whole village and are part of its set of beliefs and tradition. Most villagers follow the ceremonies step by step and play an active role. Nor is the *fiesta* a show for visitors, since they come from nearby villages (Patamban, San José de Gracia), know the people of Ocumicho, and are invited to participate. Attendance by outside individuals—tourists, officials working in the areas of tourism and arts and crafts—is extremely small.

The most important *fiesta* is that of Saint Peter and Saint Paul, since the former is the village patron. The focal activity is the procession, but firework castles and small bulls are lit, and two bands, which vie with each other all night long, are hired to play classic works. The images of Saint Peter and Saint Paul are carefully dressed and adorned for the procession with wax and plastic fruit and vegetables. Saint Peter carries a corncob, the peasants' daily food. But the saints' procession is not a purely formal act, repeated in order to carry on a tradition. In the procession of June 1979, as they came out of the church, the images were turned backward in punishment because they had not brought rain for two months and crops were wilting. The village people offer gifts to the saints—bread, fruit, and candies—and dance before their images to invoke their favor, but their attitude is not one of devoted submission, and they do not confine themselves to obey what the church dictates; they also intervene in and react to events, changing the meaning of rituals.

The relationship of the village to the outside world, its problems of survival, and the significance of *bracerismo* can be seen in one detail: women *cargueras*, who wear special costumes for the *fiesta*, carry Mexican and dollar bills tied to the multicolor ribbons that hang from their hair. These are presents that members of the *barrio* give *cargueros* to help them with *fiesta* expenses. The money comes from those who have been to the United States as *braceros* (day laborers). On the one hand, the introduction of money as an decorative element, one that participates in the *fiesta* (as a social relation, it has been part of it for a long time), reflects the social and cultural differences that have arisen in the village: depending on the amount of the gift and the contribution in kind or in currency from another country. On the other hand, it reveals that even those individuals who have left Ocumicho and share alternative life-styles abroad do come back and participate in the *fiesta*. The presence of foreign currency, which might be interpreted as a loss of Tarascan or national cultural expression, indicates a degree of ceremonial readap-tation, a new state for a torn community that finds in the *fiesta* a means to reassert those elements of its identity that come from the past and, in changes, a way to update the representation of its hardships and inequalities as well as its historical cohesion.

What does it mean when money, apart from being used to finance *fiesta* expenses, confines its appearance to a decorative, euphemized presence and commercial activity is minimal, for only ten stalls with plastic toys, decorations, and target practice games are allowed in the *plaza*? We believe that such limitations to the *fiesta* represent the relative control that the village still exercises over the commercial dependence imposed from outside, which has agents working among them. The community's Indian authorities, who are above the civic and political government where the organization of the *fiesta* is concerned, work to prevent the celebration from becoming predominantly commercial in character; thus, they also ban the introduction of arcade games. At the same time, they pressure better-off villagers to assume responsibility for the *cargueros*, thereby making those who have managed to accumulate some capital reinvest it in Ocumicho: while this *expense* does not eliminate inequality since it does not entail redistribution, it prevents any surplus obtained from village labor from being invested outside, thus intensifying the subordination to the national market.

Perhaps this control over commercial activity, its partial limitation to symbolic transactions, might represent, like artisanal production, the final efforts to survive. How much will it help them to do so from the realm of the imaginary? How effective socially will the symbolic turn out to be? For how long will they recognize themselves in what they are doing?

I asked an artisan from Ocumicho why in one of his works there were several devils huddled together, knocking each other down to get a look at themselves in a mirror. His reply was: "The mirror is appearance. You look into the mirror and you are there. You take the mirror away and you are no longer there."

The *Fiesta* in Patamban: Nondurable Crafts, Chronic Needs

Consider two settings. First, there is the concentrated space of the *plaza*, where there is trading in crafts and manufactured goods, entertainment, informal chatty meals, and arcade and chance games. At the same time, there is the itinerant space of the procession, a walk of 4 miles that begins around the center, then leaves the town, climbing the hill for the High Mass. There is a movement between the economic and the religious: on the one hand, crafts are sold in the *plaza* for a living; on the other, nondurable crafts (paper decorations hanging between houses, paths covered with patterns created with sawdust and flowers), which cover the procession route and beyond the village, up to where the hill stands, vanishing on the way back under the steps of those who carry the saint.

According to the priest in Patamban, the *fiesta* was created some fifteen to twenty years ago by an earlier priest in order to attract visitors and to promote the sale of crafts. For that reason, he arranged the decoration of the streets and the church with panels of fresh flowers, wooden arches covered with flowers and fruit, and *composturas*—paper structures that hang from strings and fill the visual space of the streets. Other informants considered the *fiesta* to be twenty to thirty years old and said that it was created for religious reasons; according to them, the introduction of commercial elements came several years after its creation.

In contrast to the patron saints' *fiestas* in Patamban, Ocumicho, and other villages, the one of Christ the King involves everyone, not just *cargueros*. The priest, nuns, and representatives from each *barrio* are in charge of its organization, but everybody participates fully in all tasks: one *barrio* is responsible for making the castle, another for the music, a third for decorating the church. Everyone makes and arranges the decorations, organized by blocks: they meet to agree on the shape, color, and materials to be used for the *composturas* and panels, suggest alternative designs, and discuss them. Most of the shapes are geometric and others copy natural forms: flowers, fruit, and corncobs. We might say, in the terms of artistic vanguards, that this is art of the poor—collective, urban, and transient.

In the past, panels were made only with fresh flowers, which were plentiful around the village. With the lower rainfall, many use sawdust, which they obtain free or very cheaply from village sawmills that cut down trees in nearby woods, though flowers are still very common. In 1977, there was a merchants' movement to change the date of the *fiesta*, designated for the last Sunday in October, to December, when a greater number of tourists might come; virtually the entire village rejected the change on the grounds that since the October date had been chosen because it was a time of abundant flowers—it had not even followed the religious calendar—then it should not be changed for commercial reasons.

Flowers, sawdust, pottery, corn: the *fiesta* prolongs the daily life and work of the village. Some agricultural activities are interrupted, but artisanal production increases at the prospect of additional sales, and people work harder than ever preparing the decorations. We can say that production changes, but not that the *fiesta* represents an escape from routine or the passage from the profane to the sacred. As in other religious *fiestas*—for example, the one in Ocumicho, which does not have commercial objectives—whatever exceptional elements in time, space, and practices there might be are always integrated within a profound continuity of the regular order of things. Materials and designs used in decorations are rooted in their working life, in common needs, and tastes. It is significant, in this respect, with which "modern" materials they chose to work. Many garlands are made with drinking straws (with which they create diamond and other elaborate shapes) and aesthetically cut-out plastic cups: when, at one point, I saw an entire block decorated in this fashion and a small boy went by carrying two pails of water, I understood the meaning. Just as—I learned later—Coca Cola bottles are used in some processions to carry candles, or simply clutched in an act of devotion, the use of straws and cups represents the role that commercial soft drinks play in a village where there are only two places to fetch water and at certain times of the year there is not enough to drink. When one goes into many of the houses, one gets the impression that they are small grocery stores, because there are four and five crates of soft drinks. Decorations made with such materials indicate not only the penetration by multinational enterprises and their plastic culture: the partial substitution, in the space of the *fiesta*, of natural materials and local pottery by others of external manufactured origin (symbolic in turn of the replacement for water), also represents the place the village allocates to them within its imaginary system and the role it gives these imported objects—similar to that of vegetables and fruit—in the material satisfaction of its needs and in invocations to power, as "mediators" in the symbolic resolution of their hardships.

Stalls selling crafts, manufactured goods, and most of the entertainment are set up in the *plaza*. The sale of crafts made in Patamban is one of the leading commercial activities: 75 percent of the population makes earthenware, and this *fiesta* gives them the opportunity to sell it in the village without incurring the cost of transport and lodging that they face the rest of the year when they travel to distant fairs or markets. Hence, weeks in advance, the whole family works to prepare a greater quantity than normal. Not all potters exhibit their ceramics in the *plaza*, because they must meet certain quality standards. Those who make ordinary earthenware recognize that the *plaza* is not the place for them, and they sell by their doorstep or simply put it away. There are also others who do not come to sell on the day of the *fiesta* because they make quality pottery by commission.

While the production and sale of local crafts remains constant, every year there are more stalls with ceramics from Ocumicho, some from San José de Gracia, and merchants trading pottery from Santa Fe de la Laguna and Guanajuato. There is an even greater number of traders who bring earthenware from cities (Zamora, Morelia, and Mexico City) and display a mixture of handmade blouses and *jorongos* from other villages and manufactured goods: shoes, clothes, household goods, and plastic and wooden trinkets (toys, combs, bracelets, necklaces, earrings, mirrors, etc.). The fair also includes stalls with vegetables, fruit, bread, candies, drinks, and snacks, which altogether make this village *fiesta* the one that attracts the most commercial activity.

A large part of the entertainment is found in the *plaza* and surrounding streets. The wheel of fortune, roundabouts, bingo that resonates through the space with its music and announcements of winning cards over loudspeakers, games of chance and skill, all brought from Zamora, make the most of this occasion, the only religious *fiesta* when they are allowed to come into the village. On all other occasions, the residents of Patamban believe that the festive period should be one of retreat; on this particular one, on the other hand, according to the priest, the joy that comes from making the highest sales of the year harmonizes with the joy from the triumph of Christ, and that atmosphere prevails in all activities. The procession itself, which moves along a path of *composturas* and multicolored panels, accompanied by bands and fireworks throughout its course, does not include burdens to be carried or mortifications, and it does not carry the kind of excessively heavy images or offerings that I witnessed in others.

However, the convergence of these elements—decorations with flowers and sawdust, music, and fireworks—does not have a merely decorative and recreational meaning, as in secularized urban *fiestas*. All the ingredients of the peasant *fiesta* serve, at the same time, a ritual movement that invokes superhuman powers and asks for their protection. The bands play Christian hymns, which the people in the procession sing, led by nuns with portable loudspeakers. Alongside it, the *coheteros* send their messages of sound and light up into the sky to please the gods of Rain and Thunder, and propiatiate their watching over the crops. During the very march to the hill, pre-Columbian and Christian gods, canticles learned in colonial times, the loudspeaker purchased three years ago, the flowers that their woods have given them for centuries, and the sawdust they now color with chemically prepared anilines, are all entwined. Thus manifested is syncretism, a crossing of cultures: Tarascan magic, Catholic religion and capitalist technology, work and prayer. That is how villages walk when one kind of domination is superimposed on another.

From a very early hour, the bands wandered the streets at various times throughout the day. They approached people who were putting up decorations in houses or on the ground, and asked them what type of music they would like to hear. Another musical event was the *pirekuas* contest, organized by the *fiesta* committee and the priest with help from the Indigenista National Institute and the Office for Tourism in awarding prizes. FONART sponsored a crafts competition: in 1979, they awarded prizes that ranged from 500 ($40) to 1,500 pesos ($120)— amounts that sometimes covered the cost of the individual piece and in a few cases were twice as high. The items entered had been on show, but as soon as the competition—which took place on the Saturday evening before the *fiesta*—was over, FONART took away the winning works as well as any of the ones displayed that it was interested in purchasing. At first, the competition had been announced for Sunday, but it was moved forward because FONART wanted to take the merchandise away as soon as possible and the following day the decorations and panels would obstruct its trucks. Many artisans who had made articles to sell in the *plaza* on the day of the *fiesta* disposed of them before the trading began. Since only twenty-four potters took part in the competition and there were no artisans among the panel of judges (which consisted of representatives from FONART, the INI, and the Casa de Artesanías in Morelia), most villagers simply watched the events. The competition in which its work was judged and given awards represented for virtually the entire village a pastime to which they had been invited only as spectators.

Seventy Thousand Tourists Created a Photogenic Culture in Janitzio

There is only one street on the island. It starts at the jetty and winds and climbs to the monument to Morelos: every shack on either side has been turned into a crafts or food stall. In the past, Janitzio had produced wood carvings and pottery, as well as *charal* (a lake fish) and whitefish—one of the most expensive in the country. Now the villagers sell crafts from many different regions, together with earthenware and clothing, and continue to make decorative objects with local images (toy boats and nets, some masks, miniature reproductions of Morelos's statue). The few surviving workshops have been turned into living exhibits to captivate tourists.

Fishing has ceased to be a collective activity for quite some time now, and the owners of large and medium-sized boats keep fishermen away from the piers, with the use of force if necessary. "Come in, eat whitefish from Pátzcuaro," they cry from the doors of the island's restaurants, but in fact what they serve at the table comes from Lake Chapala, almost 220 miles away, because the fish from the lake around Janitzio, tastier and more tender, is sent to four-star restaurants in Mexico City and Acapulco.

The crafts, the fish, and the way of life are not the island's any more. Janitzio is a giant make-believe venture. The place where Tarascan culture is best preserved is the cemetery. As in Jarácuaro, the largest island in the lake—and others with few inhabitants, like Ihuatzio, Tzurumutaro, and virtually all the villages in the region—on the nights of October 31 and November 1, the villagers visit the cemetery and take burning candles and incense. *Guares* carry the *huatzallari*, an arch decorated with yellow flowers, from which hang sugar shapes, bread, and fruit. Since precolonial times, they have placed on the ground graves elaborate *kenecuas*, offerings of bread, *chayotes*, and squash, or food previously enjoyed by the deceased. At one time, they believed that the latter came to visit them at dawn to thank them for their prayers of mediation and to protect them. Christianizing weakened such belief and infiltrated it with its own principles; secularization has gradually erased it. When asked about the meaning of the ceremony, almost all replied that "in another age" it used to be like that. It would seem that the ritual is sustained less by belief than to serve as a means of communication and symbolic production around a relationship to the unknown that social development has commercialized but has not been able to replace.

In Ihuatzio and other villages, the whole family might keep vigil over the graves, though some women do it by themselves. In Janitzio, the village men do not go into the cemetery until dawn, but tourists—seventy thousand came in 1979—do not observe this custom. To my knowledge, this has never given rise to conflict, but I have heard it said proudly how often the island has been sung about, photographed, and filmed. The light from the candles is by now as much a customary part of the ceremony as the brightness of flashlights; mourning songs blend continuously with whispers in English, French, and German.

At a time when belief is subsiding, ceremonial elements survive with a change in function. The event lost, there remain symbols—candles, arches, offerings—that economic necessity justifies otherwise. Newspapers, television, and the Office for Tourism emphasize the "profound mystical attitude" of the people, the "sacred calm of their faces," that "sadness of an entire race which turns inwards into itself";[3] they say this precisely in those brochures that urge the crowds to pounce on these *fiestas* and break the sacred or any other calm, making those who celebrate come out of themselves and try to find compensation for that which is taken from them the rest of the year.

Janitzio constitutes an extreme case of this tendency in capitalist modernization to secularize traditional events while rescuing their symbols if they can lead to higher profits. It is the same tendency that adds fairs to ancient *fiestas* or creates new *fiestas* so that fairs can have their own stage. Traders with arcade games and games of chance, bands from the cities and drinks made by big international companies, poor-quality clothing and fake crafts do the round of *fiestas* and fill the economic, symbolic, visual, and auditory space that once belonged to the regular residents of those villages. The ingredients of the traditional *fiesta* (dances, village decorations) become one element, at times additional and decorative, of the contemporary *fiesta*. In both ancient Indian *fiestas* and colonial ones, commercial activities went hand in hand with ritual celebration and the cultural or religious event, but they were integrated into the life and needs of the region.

The Christian religion, which displaced pre-Columbian cultures, confines many processions to the interior of its churches (e.g., the Virgin of Health procession in Pátzcuaro, for four years now), and relinquishes the streets to outside merchants who set up stalls, loudspeakers, and amusement parks. Given its nature as a total aesthetic experience, the new invasion of color, light, and sound brought about by their commercial display replaces the religious *fiestas*, which, in villages, constituted the major source of public integration of sight, hearing, smell, and taste, a sensory education of the masses.

The *fiesta* becomes first a fair and then a show—an intercity, national, and even international show, depending on the distance from which tourists come. The time of communal *fiestas* has long gone; entrepreneurs came and turned them into *fiestas* for others. Spectators are distinct from actors, and professionals are in charge of organizing the entertainment. Instead of *cargueros* or *mayordomos*, a group of experts prepares the setting, the loudspeakers, the lighting, and the staging of the show. Peasants, Indians, and artisans become part of the tourist show, which must be stylized or made more entertaining. Tourists, too, become part of the show for the villagers who "go to the *plaza*" out of curiosity to see outsiders, to see something foreign. This game of alien glances can end up completely as show for an even more remote audience: the photographs for which Janitzio residents charge, films, and television, which in recent years have joined in as a "natural" part of the Day of the Dead, have turned this event, which Western philosophies regard as the most solitary in a person's life, into a mass media event.

No More Questions Asked about Death

A widow asked a sacristan if it was true that the dead really came back on the day of the dead, because she wanted to wait for her husband. The sacristan told her to wait for him and that meantime she should prepare some *aguardiente* and other things he had enjoyed eating. That night, the sacristan went by the widow's house pretending to be the deceased and asked her for money and *aguardiente*. By the time he left, he was already drunk and he stayed in the street. Next morning the woman came out of her house and found the man she believed to be her husband in the street. "You are a demon . . . This man has deceived me." She took a stick and beat the sacristan, who fled. Since that day the woman has not asked any questions about the dead.[4]

I collected several tales that indicate mistrust, or outright disbelief, toward traditional beliefs and institutions and persons who represent them, but none were so paradigmatic as this one obtained by Pedro Carrasco during his research among Tarascans, which, however, he never analyzed in detail.

What is the starting point of this tale? "A widow asked a sacristan if it was true that the dead really came back on the day of the dead, because she wanted to wait for her husband." The story begins with a question that expresses doubts about traditional beliefs. The doubt concerns the possibility of restoring a beloved relationship from the past. In other words, the tale opens with a twofold movement: a desire to return to a lost state and disbelief about the redress proclaimed in the myth. The tension between these movements—past and future, what has been lost and what has been promised, the unsuspecting question and the doubt—sums up the wavering involved in the process of transition from which the story comes.

In a second stage, the religious authority guarantees the hoped-for restoration and states the requirements necessary for it to take place: "The sacristan told her to wait for him and that meantime she should prepare some *aguardiente* and other things he had enjoyed eating." The requirements mention two general needs (thirst and hunger), which, satisfied in a way common for any one member of the community (*aguardiente* and the "things he had enjoyed eating"), create the ambiguity necessary to apply either to the husband or the priest.

The third phrase justifies the original doubt; it discredits hope and reveals the motive for the deceit. "That night, the sacristan went by the widow's house pretending to be the deceased and asked her for money and *aguardiente*." There are two changes between the early ritual demands and what is required when they have to be met: in the second instance, the sacristan does not request food, that is to say, the most essential element, the most legitimate part of the offering, is gone; instead, besides *aguardiente*, he asks for money: the fraud is associated with exploitation and alcoholism. "By the time he left, he was already drunk and he stayed in the street."

The woman finds him when she "comes out of her house" (she attains knowledge as she leaves the domestic world), and curses and beats up the sacristan, who is now referred to as just a "man" rather than by his religious office. The conclusion does not state whether the woman has stopped believing in the church, priests, or the mythology of mourning. With a much more thought-provoking, literarily magnificent turn, it asserts that "since that day the woman has not asked any questions about the dead." It is not merely a question of the loss of a particular belief, but of a radical change in the structure of thought: it discovers areas about which no questions should be asked if one does not wish to be deceived.

However, who are the dead, what is dead, about which no questions must be asked? If we link this story with the tactics of survival and economic speculation developed in the festivity, we find that the precise fact of the physical death of beloved relatives and friends can be taken, as in any other culture, as a metaphor for other losses. Dead is what has gone within and around oneself, in the society in which we live: people, and also customs, social relations, objects.

Faced with loss of the belief in the return of the dead, and in the offerings to invoke them, because of "money," Tarascans commercialize their celebration, they "revive" rituals in order to take advantage of the money economy that assails them. Of course, we are not dealing with an original decision, as we have to acknowledge the encroaching initiative of the capitalist economy and culture at the start of the commercialization of the *fiestas*. But there are a series of acts generated by the village itself, particularly in Janitzio, which have contributed to the commercialization of the *fiesta*: setting up food and drink stalls throughout the island, adapting crafts and ceremonies, demanding payment to be photographed and filmed.

The death of the belief in death, as understood by their ancestors, is transformed into a life, or at least a survival, strategy, though such responses involve the ambivalence of favoring village interests while at the same time subordinating the village to an exploitative economic regime. This regime does not just control and destroy them from outside; it also kills communal life as it reproduces itself within it, promoting the accumulation of capital by a small privileged sector (merchants, boatmen, fish, and craft profiteers). When no more questions are asked about death, will it not be necessary to address another question mark, to inquire why the village is not allowed to turn death into life, why one part of the village begins to destroy the other?

The *Fiesta* as Limited Subversion

The *fiestas* studied reflect, symbolically and materially, the changes undergone by the villages that hold them. They represent the state of conflicts between traditional peasant production—which until recently was a subsistence economy, centered around the household, governed by the logic of use value—and its gradual incorporation into the capitalist market. The weakening of their ancient structures and ceremonies, their substitution, additions, or refunctionalization by "modern" agents are staged in the hybrid nature of the *fiesta*. Changes to dances and decorations, their coexistence with urban shows and entertainment, reveal impositions from those who control them but are also attempts to restructure them and link the past to their current contradictions.

As a global phenomenon, which incorporates every aspect of social life, the *fiesta* reveals the role of economic, political, religious, and aesthetic elements in the process of continuity-transformation of popular culture. We have seen that rituals, their recurrence, extinction, and innovation, can be interpreted as attempts to intervene in the remodeling of their social structures, to preserve endogenous control over life in the village (Ocumicho) or reform it such that it conforms to the outside order (the national market and tourism in Janitzio).

There is, therefore, continuity between the *fiesta* and ordinary life, between what we Westerners differentiate as religious and profane. Ceremonial acts cannot be separated from ordinary ones. Both in the *sierra* villages (Patamban, Ocumicho) as in those by the lake (Ihuatzio, Tzintzuntzan), saints' images are kept with equal devotion in churches and in the houses of *cargueros* and *barrio* leaders. R. A. M. van Zantwijk has remarked, "People deal with the gods almost in the same manner that they deal with prominent and influential individuals in their social sphere. There is no fundamental difference between the way in which they greet a *jefe*, a *principal* (elder) or a *pasado* (former elder) and the way in which they talk to saints: at the most there would be a difference in the degree of dignity."[5]

The continuity shown between work time and *fiesta* time, between everyday and ceremonial events and the manner in which the organization of labor (familial and by *barrio*) extends to the preparations for the festivities displaces all absolute opposition between the *fiesta* and daily life. It also leads us to suspect the craftiness with which dualist conceptions have distorted data about other *fiestas* to "legitimize" their distinction between ceremonies and the material, everyday conditions that give rise to them.

We did not find among the cases studied, nor among other Michoacán *fiestas*—patron saints', Holy Week, civic, or urban—the possibility of using the notion of the *fiesta* as an "escape from ordinary time," which, impressed by its tiresome reiteration in the bibliography, we brought to the field as a hypothesis.

To what do *fiestas* make reference? Not to the sacred Grand Time or to hallowed mysteries, but to times of sowing, to harvests and rains, to the common needs for food and health, to the order that structures their habits and their hopes. Why do they hold *fiestas*? To preserve that order, to restore it, or to relocate themselves in a new one, as they uncover it through, primarily, their economic practices: the growth or decline of produce, the sale of crafts, unemployment, migration. They hold them, also, to consolidate emotional communal relations and the sense of belonging of those who have left and now return to join in the celebrations. A forced internal reinvestment of the economic surplus, a controlled catharsis of those elements that cannot erupt under oppressed labor but that are also controlled during the festive incursion to prevent any threat to permanent cohesion: the *fiesta* is not an outrageous liberation of instincts, as so many phenomenologists and anthropologists have thought, but a demarcated place and time in which the rich must pay for everybody's pleasure and in which everybody's pleasure is moderated by "social interest." The parodies of power, the irreverent questioning of order (even in carnivals) are tolerated in spaces and times that do not threaten the subsequent return to "normality." Discontinuity and exceptionality lead back to routine, they constitute the exact opposite of and a compensation for what they do not have, but within the norms established by the ordinary authorities (*cargueros, mayordomos, priests*). In Janitizio, Patamban, and other villages, one sees that the extraordinary elements that they hope for during *fiestas* involve the amount of sales of food and crafts, and a chance to buy manufactured goods and to amuse themselves with arcade games that are not normally found in the *plazas.*

Having offered such a social account of the *fiesta,* I am not, however, forgetting that ceremonies with Indian roots still incorporate beliefs about the relationship to nature and to transcendental entities that withstand reduction to contemporary economic determinations. Pre-Columbian rituals and dances and some Catholic processions come out of historical experiences when popular identity was shaped and they represent—with a certain degree of ambiguity—that area of culture that resists being turned into a commercial show and that does not trust the promises of the capitalist market or tourism. With regard to the pilgrim-age to Chalma, Gilberto Giménez remarked that the survival of noncapitalist commemorative elements reveals a regressive and utopian aspect: the aspiration to revitalize periodically a lost communal unity and the hope to reconquer a self-sufficient way of life.[6] The ambivalent and contradictory way of bringing the present together with the past and the future enables different *fiestas,* or separate social sectors within the same *fiesta,* to attribute alternative meanings to these relations with the transcendental realm: a ritual can be evasive or liberating. There are no dances or ceremonies inevitably anesthetizing or challenging; in every case, we must examine their meaning for participants and spectators, depending on the particular context or conjuncture. And, above all, we must remember that—counter to the reduction of religious elements to mere ideology, which recognizes only its cognitive aspect, therefore its distortion—religious *fiestas* also have political and psychosocial func-tions: of cohesion, resignation, catharsis, growth, and collective rein-forcement.

In a sense, it is clear that religious ideology and ritual remove individuals from reality and from the present. Rituals seem to work in nature and society, but they really act on their representations: their working at the level of symbols[7] can be effective when the cause of harm—as in the case of certain diseases—lies in the psychic or cultural realm, but we know it is useless, that its effect is illusory, when it seeks to change something that is strictly material, such as drought. We can also add that religious ritual is an instrument for *regulating* and *postpon-ing*: it consigns unsatisfied needs to fictitious places and times, it governs their staging, their controlled eruption, their masked sublima-tion in the dance, the procession, the games, through duties and rules. However, the *fiesta* offers an opportunity to lift certain daily restric-tions, a chance for bodies to become aware of, and express, their role-playing power: the strictest ritual, particularly if it is a collective one, opens up society to—as Roberto de Matta wrote with reference to the Brazilian carnival— "an alternative view of itself . . . to invent a new world through the dramatization of our social reality."[8] Whether resignation or the emergence of desire prevails in the *fiesta* will depend on the relationship between the repressive and expressive forces within each society.

What is the fate of the traditional beliefs that gave rise to *fiestas*? The secularization and commercialization of ceremonies is in reverse proportion to the extent to which a community is well integrated and has succeeded in satisfying its basic needs. For example, the disintegrating effects of tourism on an Indian celebration, family structure, or daily habits will be greater where unemployment drives many villagers to seek outside work or to adapt their cultural norms and products to external codes in order to obtain the necessary means to survive.

The prevailing tendency in capitalist modernization is to reduce, or nullify, the difference between rural participatory *fiestas* and urban commercial shows, as another consequence of the subordination of the countryside to the city, of local life to the national and multinational market. Let us express it better with the help of Michel Freitag and Marianne Mesnil: it is increasingly harder to distinguish rural from urban, traditional beliefs and habits, and autonomous forms of organization, from those controlled from the industrial city, whose decision-making center surpasses individual urban settlements. We live in a "supraurban productive system" that replaces the opposition between city and countryside with a homogenized economic, political, and cultural restructuring.[9]

Nevertheless, supraurban expansion and its need to standardize production and consumption find certain limitations in the specific configuration of each culture and in the interest of the system itself to sustain ancient forms of social organization and representation. We can see with regard to *fiestas*, too, how—due to economic (to retain additional sources of work, such as crafts), political (to use *cacicazgo* or other traditional mechanisms of authoritarian power), or ideological (to consolidate a national identity, to keep "living museums" in order to attract tourists) reasons—the dominant culture preserves archaic pockets, conferring on them new functions and new contexts.

What is needed to prevent the popular *fiesta* from becoming completely lost within a show, to continue to be centered around communal life, providing a space and time for collective participation? Can it still strenghthen cultural identity and contribute to the reconstruction of social cohesion? This is possible if the village manages to make sure that expansion, satisfaction, and expenditure are carried out according to internal standards, or that at least they are not subordinated to the interests of big commercial capital. This occurs if the villagers retain a major role in material and symbolic organization, if they assure through the cargo system the reinvestment of the economic surplus of production in the financing of the festivities, or if, in the case of *fiestas* that have national repercussions, such as those in large ceremonial centers, they secure a decisive role in the governmental, tourist, and artisanal institutions that program these events and are in a position to control the penetration of external agents. It is self-evident to add that in order to achieve this, villages must organize themselves and must do so democratically. Otherwise, soft drinks and beer companies, traders of manufactured goods, and urban forms of entertainment will continue to take away from Indian groups—at times with the connivance of inside leaders—the space and meaning of their *fiestas*, the places and times that they have chosen for remembrance or joy.

Conclusion: Toward a Popular Culture in Small Letters

The Interpenetration of Cultures and the Definition of Popular

We have said that almost everything that is done with crafts alternates between market and museum, between commercialization and conservation. However, in some sense, nothing is more unlike a museum than life under capitalism. There was a time when the arrangement of display cases, the formal and peaceful placing of objects, corresponded to the outside world. Born in Europe to store away the booty from conquests, museums reproduced in their classifications the appropriation by the bourgeoisie of societies and their objects, the places allocated to them. A king or a president could stroll through the colonies like a tourist through the rooms of a museum: over there, the countries that produced raw materials; over here, those that processed them. The former, locked into a familiar and cyclical bond with nature, simply repeated myths, *fiestas*, and dances as monotonous as nature itself; Western ones, on the other hand, seduced by economic and technological expansion, had made invention the motivating force of a culture undergoing constant renewal and growth. There were educational missions that sought to pass on to a few of the colonized the Culture, the "higher" codes necessary for exotic societies to understand their place in the world. But this glance, benevolent and contemptuous all at once, reinforced the difference. The hierarchical gesture of the educator guaranteed that culture and barbarism would not be confused. Each would be in its own display case.

The growth of the market brought this impeccable order to an end. The dominant classes, which excluded subordinate ones both from the production and consumption of certain ideological goods, had to change their ideology and practices in part: they continued to exclude the people from having control over production, but in order to expand sales, they allowed large sectors to have access to the consumption of many cultural products. Thus, manufactured goods replaced crafts in Indian and mestizo villages. The socioeconomic and cultural rise of the popular classes, their demands to participate in "modern" consumption converge, in a sense, with the need to expand the market. Although, of course, the economic and political struggles of classes, ethnic enclaves, and subordinated nations represent the main challenge to the imposed order.

The response of capitalism has been, endless times, repression. However, the most ordinary and incisive answer attempts to incorporate popular cultures, integrate them, and give a new meaning to their messages and a new function to their objects. In urban craft shops, in museums, in advertising and tourism, as we have seen, subordinate representations and practices are restructured in order to make them compatible, so that they might even contribute to the development of the hegemonic system. The dominant culture becomes internalized in popular habits, the ethnic is reduced to the typical, and the various strategies of survival tried by the oppressed classes are standardized in order to subordinate them to the global organization of the symbolic realm. Other very subtle factors are at work in this process: the need to renew demand led industrial businesses to apply Indian designs, and bourgeois "nationalist" sectors and artists interested in popular dissemination and subjects to incorporate messages from the subordinate classes in elite circles. The outcome is an intersecting, an interpenetration of objects and symbolic systems.

Our study of these movements of transference and interaction between cultures, of mixed formations, confirmed the problem pointed out at the beginning of defining the popular according to certain intrinsic qualities: crafts because they are handmade, *fiestas* because of their ceremonial nature, popular culture, in short, because of its peasant or Indian or "traditional" origins. As has often been remarked, all these labels—just like the term *folklore*—originated in industrial societies, as part of the classifying Eurocentrism that is always anxious to subject reality to the meticulous world of museums.

The popular, therefore, cannot in my view denote a set of objects (crafts or Indian dances), only a position and an action. We cannot narrow it down to a particular type of goods or messages, because the sense of one or the other is constantly altered by social conflicts. The fact that an object has been produced by the people or is consumed avidly by them does not guarantee its popular character forever; popular meaning and value are gained in social relations. It is use, not origin, the position and capacity to arouse popular acts and representations that confer that quality.

Similarly, crafts, which might once have been identified by the way in which they were produced (before the industrial revolution, everything was handmade), today must include in their characterization the social process through which they move, from the time of production to the time of consumption. In part, the term *artisanal* continues to denote a particular way of using implements, but their meaning is also formed by their reception, through a series of features attributed to objects (age, primitivism, etc.), though they may have been produced with industrial technology.

Popular Art, Kitsch Art, or Popular Culture?

Some writers sought to rid themselves of these uncertainties by talking of popular art. This name, which always includes a significant share of romanticism, isolates *one* aspect in the production of *a few* individual pieces—creativity—and attempts to make it *the* distinctive criterion to define and assess what is Indian. Almost everyone who does this smuggles into the area of what is popular the concept of art developed among Western aesthetics doctrines of the last four centuries: a concept based on the predominance of form over function and on the autonomy of objects. It is natural that they should feel that many rustic crafts, imperfectly finished and available for popular consumption, do not deserve to be called art. If we could free the concept from its elitist and Eurocentric connotation, if we could expand it to incorporate non-Western aesthetic forms, such as Indian ones, we would be able to include under the name of art expressions that handle in a different manner the tangible and imaginary relations of individuals with other individuals and with their environment.[1]

As long as we fail do this, our conceptualizations of popular art will force objects to fit into classifications alien to their meaning, and will underestimate many of them, because they do not "fit" in musems, into the world of *kitsch*. Under this rubric, which has no equivalent among us and which addresses us from one of the languages of domination, are included common or "useless" objects given an artistic coating, untidily finished crafts decorated with iconography or colors that shock our cultured sensitivity, and many atypical usages or copies that the popular classes make of goods of the grand Culture. This idea, which, significantly, originated in Munich about 1869, together with a certain increase in bourgeois well-being and the growth of mechanical methods of mass reproduction, serves to preserve, and acts as a customhouse for, "good taste." The hegemonic system, which needs to expand economically and ideologically and must respond to consumer demands with available and commercial adaptations of goods and symbols extolled by the bourgeoisie, defended itself, pronouncing as fake the taste and manners of those who wanted to share its privileges. "Art and kitsch are two necessary and interdependent terms in the economic and conceptual realm... The inaccessibility of artistic 'essences' is measured by the amount of failed imitations which they invite. Hence the reason for the existence of kitsch, the notion of kitsch: the more there is of it the more the authenticity of 'art' will shine; the more widespread it becomes, the more the aristocratic character of the possessor of 'art' will stand out."[2]

A further reason for the existence in Latin America of what is regarded as kitsch is the commercial demand to produce copies of pre-Columbian designs but to adapt them to modern aesthetic standards, or, to be more precise, to those of the middle sectors. That is how what Alberto Beltrán has called "Neopre-Hispanic art" spread. *Neo* and *pre*: the irony comes from the real contradictions that commercial speculation provokes in the area of artisanal production, rather than from some linguistic game. The essence of what is considered kitsch is not found primarily in objects; it is the style with which the capitalist market relates to the popular. The parody does not lie with individual pieces (popular and petit-bourgeois consumers place them in their homes, seriously convinced of their beauty); what is parodylike or grotesque is the effect of a particular kind of reception and is the attempt of the hegemonic classes to distance themselves from what they themselves have brought about.

In order to abrogate this choice between art and kitsch, we must vindicate popular culture, the most diverse products, and their most heterodox usages. I am not suggesting an indiscriminate aesthetic vindication, like populism, which decrees everything popular as good and beautiful simply because it is done by the people, and ignores that many of their objects, practices, and tastes are second-hand adaptations of the culture that oppresses them. What I mean is a scientific and political vindication, abolishing the criteria for inclusion imposed by art histories, aesthetic doctrines, and folklore, opening those disciplines to a critical, unbiased analysis of popular tastes and uses according to their representativity and social value.

If I prefer to talk of culture instead of popular art, it is because the beauty, creativity, or authenticity of popular events is not my primary concern; my main interest lies in what Cirese has called "their sociocultural representativity," in other words, the fact that they indicate the ways and means with which certain social classes have lived cultural life in relation to their real conditions of existence as subordinate classes.[3] However, to avoid interpreting this scientific definition in a nondynamic fashion, as a simple reference to the "(objective) conditions of existence," though I am aware that this was not Cirese's intention, it seems useful to add Brecht's political characterization:

Popular is that which the vast masses understand/that which gathers and enriches their form of expression/it is that which incorporates and reaffirms their viewpoint/it is that which is so representative of the most progressive section of the people that it can take over leadership and also be comprehensible to the other sectors/it is what, setting out from tradition, carries it forward/ what it conveys to the sector of the people which aspires to power/ the gains of the sector which at present sustains it.[4]

What matters for a fact or an object to be popular is how popular sectors use it rather than its place of origin (an Indian community or a music academy), or the presence or absence of folkloric symbols (rusticity or the image of a pre-Columbian god). Let us add a paradox: earthenware from Tlaquepaque, in Guadalajara, produced by Jalisco artisans inspired by archaic designs but working in workshops owned by American business executives, where they submit to their stylistic modifications and lose economic and symbolic control of the work through selling to tourists, does not constitute popular art. On the other hand, a masterpiece by Goya, undertaken by Indian and mestizo peasants from Aranza, in Michoacán, with the aid of artists from the Taller de Investigación Plástica de Morelia (the Workshop for Plastic Arts Research of Morelia), to make a mural that addresses community problems from their perspective, does.

Cultural Policies and Self-management: Basis and Contradictions

This conception of the popular helps to state precisely the direction that cultural policies seeking to promote it must take. If the popular is not defined by its beauty or its authenticity, its top priority is not the cultivation of its artistic dignity or the preservation of its authenticity (which are also valuable). We have already criticized such a romantic, *conservative*, conception, which sees only the cultural, or purely aesthetic, question and devotes itself to safeguarding traditions and to preserving the designs, techniques, and the social relations with which Indians once identified themselves.

Neither do we accept the opposite position, *developmentalist technocratism*: escaping into what it imagines to be the optimum future, it proposes modernizing the production and design of crafts, or simply abolishing them and incorporating Indians into industrial production. As far as *fiestas* are concerned, this position seeks to readjust them to the aesthetic and recreational habits of tourism, to turn them into mass shows, or to replace them with arcade games and modern dances. From the domestic workshop to the factory, from the sale of their products at depreciated prices in the peasant market to their sale for export or in the urban shop at depreciated prices, exploitation barely changes stages. There is an overwhelming disproportion between the profits that modernization can bring producers and the deculturation suffered by them as they lose the familial organization of labor, communal land ownership, and other mainstays of their identity. The developmentalist pledge to improve the condition of artisans by turning them into proletarians or offering them a new subordinate role within a different kind of exploitation is a very unimaginative version of similar old stratagems, whose level of conjuring qualifies them to be included alongside those ridiculed by Borges in his *Historia universal de la infamia:* "In 1517, Father Bartolomé de las Casas took much pity on those Indians who wasted away in the gruelling infernos of Caribbean gold mines, and he proposed to the emperor Charles V the importation of Blacks, who would waste away in the gruelling infernos of Caribbean gold mines."[5]

If the option seems to lie between conservative or technocratic "solutions," it is because both represent two faces of the same system. This bifurcation in cultural policies corresponds, to a certain extent, to strategies of different sectors of the bourgeoisie. The industrial faction, which seeks economic growth through technological development, finds in crafts an obstacle that must be eradicated, remnants of precapitalist forms of production. The agrarian sector—and that element of the commercial bourgeoisie that speculates in peasant production, acts as intermediaries for artisans, or benefits from tourism—counts on the expansion of traditional resources for capital accumulation: thus, it emphasizes the ideological and folkloric role of popular cultures, and it insists on preserving its products and *fiestas* to provide peasants with an additional source of income and tourists with exotic attractions.

Apart from any political criticism for which these positions call, I must point out their conceptual aberrations. Both those who attempt to protect and preserve the independence of indigenous forms as well as those who seek only to improve production and to include crafts under the capitalist market make the mistake of divorcing the economic and the symbolic. Any solution that takes into account only one of these levels cannot resolve current conflicts of identity and survival of popular cultures.

A policy that confines itself to preserving cultural tradition (see the migration of youths and the persistent poverty of those who remain behind in the unchanged villages) or the simple economic incorporation into the capitalist market and consumption (let us think of artisans turned into proletarians working for mediocre wages for entrepreneurs who modify their cultural designs in order to make them competitive) will not satisfy artisans. If we believe that the motive behind the manufacture of crafts lies in both the continuity of a cultural tradition and the pressing need to complement low earnings from the land, it is clear that the artisanal crisis cannot be resolved in isolation from the rest of the agrarian question.

On the other hand, when we bear in mind that the rudimentary materials and methods considered by many as essential to crafts originated from an adaptation to natural surroundings and to earlier forms of social organization, there is no reason why those materials and methods cannot in turn be adapted to the new economic and cultural conditions of migrants crowded together in capital cities or living in peasant villages that have undergone changes. Would a reformulation in response to current resources and incentives of materials, processes, and designs—even the alternative that many might stop making crafts in order to go into other productive sectors that may offer them higher living standards—be inconsistent with such changes?

Questions concerning what crafts represent today or what popular culture is cannot be dissociated from others, such as why to continue producing them or for whom. Undoubtedly, these are problems that concern the state and society as a whole, questions that merge with the balance of payments, the economic budgeting necessary in a planned society, and the global direction of economic development. However, artisans, dancers, and other workers in popular culture must be the first to express their thoughts, because we are not dealing simply with a macroeconomic question. At stake are domestic and cooperative forms of petty production, cultural identity, and life-style that are to be wiped out for the sake of certain exclusive advantages of big industry that remain unclear. With due recognition for the theoretical problems and those of economic and cultural global policy that we have discussed, the answer to what crafts must represent today rests primarily with the producers themselves. The first issue to be resolved is not whether it is suitable to preserve traditional forms though it may keep them in poverty, to refine processes and improve quality in order to make them competitive with industry, or to reproduce their traditional designs in objects manufactured with new technology. The fundamental decision to be made concerns the introduction of democratic and critical participation by artisans themselves and the creation of the conditions under which they can exercise it. A cultural policy that seeks to serve the popular classes must start with an unexpected answer to the following question: What needs to be protected, crafts or artisans?

Ushering in democratic participation and creating the conditions under which they can exercise it, we must emphasize the importance of combining both aspects. To confine oneself to simply questioning the economic and political global system and its hierarchical domination often leads to populism. If there is to be a popular culture, it is not enough to remove the obstacles to collective participation, as if there were uncontaminated masses who just need to have the prison bars—external to them—removed to express themselves freely. The thought and practice of the people have also been shaped by the dominant culture (it is not only intellectuals and the bourgeoisie who are "ideologized"), with the additional burden that their century-old exclusion from education and centers of power has deprived the people of the necessary means to understand the system that oppresses them and to change it.

How can artisans, usually illiterate peasants with little or no experience in macroeconomic or intercultural issues, develop their own position on their problems without better knowledge of the place of their labor within the totality of production, the place of their ethnic enclave and their class within the national society? There is, in spite of everything, heightened awareness and critical thinking by Indians and other popular sectors, but oppression forces them to develop in isolation, fragmentation, and marginality. The vast majority of producers who attend urban markets are only looking to convert their labor into money to buy commodities that possess use value for themselves and their families; even among artisans who set up cooperatives or deal with the state, it is clear that their thinking and practices are organized around the issues of subsistence, of relations of non-profit-making reciprocity and "alliances of trust,"[6] dominant in the Indian world. Rarely discussed are the tasks necessary to challenge the system or just to accumulate capital. Whereupon the creation of "progressive value" and control of the market fall upon state agencies and private intermediaries. Certainly, there are objective economic and political causes that hinder artisan and peasant participation, but there is also an almost submissive acceptance, a habit of thinking only about the immediate pragmatic objectives of production within the narrow horizon of their village.

Many of the data gathered during my fieldwork can help to illustrate how the capitalist system reproduces its own forms of competition within subordinated ethnic enclaves and pushes Indians aside into a marginal corner to ensure, among other things, their ignorance of the laws imprisoning them. Let me offer two examples. The only attempt I came across to have an artisan as part of the panel of judges in a contest was organized by FONART and the INI in Patamban in October 1980. The woman artisan who was invited, a leader of her village and one of the most skilled, told me that she had resigned before the panel had met because she could not stand the pressure from her neighbors, that she feared some might stop greeting her and others might assault her if she did not agree to award them a prize. The hard competitive conditions, which reveal the extent to which a village hidden in the *sierra* reproduces the capitalist pattern of fighting for profit and prestige, do not work themselves out by allowing the occasional participation of producers in decision-making organs.

The other example is an artisan from Ihuatzio, who worked with rush. He told me that he had been weaving airplanes in that adobe village for a few years when he was taken to London for a month to attend an exhibition organized by the Mexican government. "What did you think of London?" "I don't know. I didn't see anything. As it was very cold, I spent the whole month sitting by this burner working." It is logical up to a point: what interest can a foreign city hold for a Tarascan who for seventy years did not leave the banks of Lake Pátzcuaro? But we might also ask ourselves how someone who is not interested in seeing London or Mexico City, or in understanding how the centers of power function, can manage to construct a consistent alternative to official strategies, to situate ethnic claims critically within the capitalist development for which he works.

There will be no truly popular cultural policies as long as producers do not play a leading role, and they will hold such a role only after a radical democratization of civil society. The necessary tasks go beyond the simple "rescuing" of collective structures and Indian traditions or a warm respect for ethnic autonomy and the rise of cooperatives or local struggles. To prevent these efforts from sinking into inefficiency or from being assimilated by the hegemonic regime as one more gear in its process of reproduction, they must transcend isolated economic or ethnic claims, weld these together, and coordinate the struggles of each individual group into interethnic political entities: national, even international, federations, capable of multiplying their strength and lending their gains a dimension appropriate to the multinational programs of capitalism. However, since the oppression of Indians is shared, in several senses, by the other popular sectors, and since ethnic power by itself will not succeed in changing the world system, Indian struggles need to join with those of organizations that represent the interests of workers, peasants, and all subordinate sectors. This means that ethnic groups, beginning with an adequate characterization of their subjection, must assign an anticapitalist (and not merely anticolonialist) meaning to their struggles, and that political parties and union movements must recognize in ethnic oppression and cultural conflicts specific problematics often neglected.

The failure of so many cooperative groups due to the fact that their members operate with economic and ideological habits contrary to their goals, the fact that many of those who work in association with others do not fare any better than those who work by themselves, and the limited change achieved within the area of artisanal production as a whole by state agencies (even in Mexico, the Latin American country with the greatest initiative and investment in this area), all show how hard it is to escape from the contradictions imposed on crafts as long as we remain within a capitalist logic. This is not to say that we must wait for the arrival of an alternative system in order to face up to these conflicts. On the contrary, while artisanal production is a type of production that shows more clearly the contradictions of the social process, it can also be a fitting ground to try out forms of socialization and to face resolutely what must die, what can be recovered through change, and what must be created in order to construct a new culture.

The conclusion must be the following: the future of popular cultures depends on the whole society. We need artisans to participate, to be critical and to organize themselves, and to redefine their production and the way they relate to the market and to consumers; but we also need to create a new public, a new tourism, an alternative way of enjoying and thinking about culture. We need a systematic change of all means of cultural production, circulation, and consumption. We must reorganize institutions devoted to artistic and artisanal promotion and distribution, construct an alternative history of art and an alternative theory of culture, alternative schools, and alternative mass media so that those cultural processes locked up inside the exhibit cases of Art can be relocated within the myriad of facts and messages amid which we learn to think and feel. However, this reorganization of the cultural realm will be fully accomplished only in a society that is not based on the commercial exploitation of men and women and their work, or at least where people fight to build such a society. If we can get crafts, dances, and *fiestas* to contribute to attaining it, if we can get them to join in with the common struggles of rural and urban life, we will be proud to write *culture* in small letters. This is the only way to stop writing it in quotation marks.

Notes

Preface

1. Michoacán is one of the regions in the country that has most consistently awakened the interest of Mexican and foreign anthropologists over time. While it has an old and established literature, already reviewed elsewhere (Lucio Mendieta y Nuñez, *Los tarascos*), truly scientific studies began with a program for anthropological research sponsored by American and Mexican institutions in the forties (D. F. Rubín de la Borbolla and Ralph L. Beals, "The Tarascan Project," pp. 708–712). That project resulted in a geographical study (Robert C. West, *Cultural Geography of the Modern Tarascan Area*), and several others on particular villages (Ralph L. Beals, *Cherán: A Sierra Tarascan Village*; George M. Foster, *Tzintzuntzan*; Donald Brand and José Correa Nuñez, *Quiroga, a Mexican Municipio*; Pedro Carrasco, *El catolicismo popular de los tarascos*, which deals particularly with the area around Lake Pátzcuaro, primarily with data gathered in Jarácuaro).

Other studies on the region that should be mentioned are those by Pierre Lise, *Las artesanías y pequeñas industrias en el estado de Michoacán*; Ina R. Dinerman, *Los tarascos, campesinos y artesanos de Michoacán*; R. A. M. van Zantwijk, *Los servidores de los santos*; George Pierre Castile, *Cherán: la adaptación de una comunidad tradicional de Michoacán*; John W. Durston, *Organización social de los mercados campesinos en el centro de Michoacán*; Victoria Novelo, *Artesanías y capitalismo en México*; Anne Lise and René Pietri, *Empleo y migración en la región de Pátzcuaro*.

1. From the Primitive to the Popular: Theories about Inequality between Cultures

1. A. Kroeber and C. Kluckhohn, *Culture. A Critical Review of Concepts and Definitions*.
2. Claude Lévi-Strauss, *Race et histoire*. (There is a Spanish translation in his *Antropología estructural*.)
3. Lévi-Strauss, *El pensamiento salvaje*, p. 24.
4. Ibid., p. 31.
5. Ibid., p. 30.
6. Ibid., p. 33.

7. Lévi-Strauss, *Race et histoire*, pp. 38–39.
8. Lucy Mair, *Native Policies in Africa.* Quoted in Gérard Leclerc, *Antropologie et colonialisme*, p. 151.
9. Quoted in Leclerc, ibid., pp. 161–163.
10. Antonio Gramsci, *El materialismo histórico y la filosofía de Benedetto Croce*, pp. 150–151.
11. Roger Establet, "Culture et idéologie," pp. 7–26.
12. Maurice Godelier has justified the structural role of elements tradition-ally regarded as ideological through the use of typically ethnological tools ("Infraestructura, sociedades e historia"). M. Diskin and S. Cook (*Mercados de Oaxaca*) and Gilberto Giménez (*Cultura popular y religión en el Anahuac*), among others, have done the same with reference to Latin America, showing that relationships of kinship and *compadrazgo* and juridical and political elements such as an agrarian reform program and the ceremonial and symbolic organiza-tion of a *fiesta* may be involved in the relations of production.
13. I have developed this point at greater length in my book *La producción simbólica. Teoría y método en sociología del arte*, chap. 3.
14. Pierre Bourdieu, *Reproduction in Education, Society and Culture*, and *Distinción: A Social Critique of the Judgement of Taste.*
15. Louis Althusser, *Ideología y aparatos ideológicos del Estado*, p. 15.
16. Bourdieu, *Reproduction in Education*, pp. 52–53.
17. On this point, see Darcy Ribeiro, *Las Américas y la civilización*, vol. 1.

2. Introduction to the Study of Popular Cultures

1. Alberto M. Cirese, *Ensayo sobre las culturas subalternas*, pp. 55–56 , 68–70.
2. Edward H. Spicer, "Acculturation," pp. 21–27.
3. Memorandum 15, International Institute of African Languages and Cul-ture. Quoted in George Pierre Castile, *Cherán*, p. 14.
4. Ralph Linton, *Acculturation in Seven American Indian Tribes.* Quoted in Castile, *Cherán*, p. 16.
5. Gonzalo Aguirre Beltrán, *El proceso de aculturación.*
6. Cirese, *Ensayo*, p. 51.
7. Ibid., p. 54.
8. L. M. Lombardi Satriani, *Apropiación y destrucción de la cultura de las clases subalternas*, pp. 77–119.
9. Giovanni Battista Bronzini, *Cultura popolare—dialettica e contestualitá*, p. 15.
10. In a later book, *Culturas híbridas*, I analyze this process in detail.
11. Novelo, *Artesanías*, p. 7.
12. Mircea Eliade, *Lo sagrado y lo profano*, p. 80.
13. Jean Duvignaud, *Fêtes et civilizations*, p. 46.
14. Ibid., p. 41.
15. Eric Wolf is among those who hold the "redistribution" thesis; Aguirre Beltrán has criticized their position and has talked instead of "leveling." Castile developed both aspects in his study of Tarascans quoted above (*Cherán*, pp. 62–66).

3. Artisanal Production as a Capitalist Necessity

1. *I Seminario sobre la problemática artesanal* (Rodolfo Becerril Straffon's contribution), FONART-SEP, 1979, p. 1.

2. Teresa Rendón, "Utilización de la mano de obra en la agricultura mexicana, 1940–1973."

3. Lise and Pietri, *Empleo y migración en Pátzcuaro*, p. 257.

4. Lise and Pietri, "La artesanía: un factor de integración del medio rural," p. 360. In the last few years, several works have characterized the Mexican peasant economy and its place within the process of capitalist development. To get acquainted with the by-now well-known theoretical arguments and empirical data, we will simply refer the reader to two recent studies: Mario Margulis, *Contradicciones en la estructura agraria y transferencia de valor*, and Armando Bartra, *La explotación del trabajo campesino por el capital*.

As for the specific organization of artisanal production in Michoacán and its place within the peasant economy, apart from the discussion in this present chapter, the reader will find further treatment of the subject in chap. 5 and in the Conclusion.

5. Gobi Stromberg, "El juego del coyote: platería y arte en Taxco," unpublished, pp. 16–17.

6. Bessie Galbraith, "Artesanía," pp. 9–12.

7. Ibid.

8. Data taken from the Plan for the Development of Tourism, Government of Michoacán, 1974–1980, vol. 1.

9. Figures from the Bank of Mexico quoted by Novelo, *Artesanías*, p. 15.

10. Manuel Gamio, *Forjando patria*, p. 183.

11. Salvador Novo, "Nuestras artes populares," p. 56. Quoted by Novelo, *Artesanías*, p. 35. See also Maria Luisa Zaldívar Guerra, *Consideraciones sobre el arte popular en México*.

12. Novelo, *Artesanías*, pp. 14–16.

13. This critique was suggested to me by the sociologist Alfredo Pucciarelli, while discussing this chapter.

4. The Fractured Society

1. Alonso de la Rea, "Crónica de la Orden de N. Seráfico P.S. Francisco, provincia de San Pedro y San Pablo de Michoacán en la Nueva España (1643)." Quoted by Durston, *Organización social*, p. 24.

2. For an analysis of changes in dances and *fiestas* through colonial times, see the book by Arturo Warman, *La danza de moros y cristianos*.

3. Godelier, "Infraestructura"; see also his book *Economía, fetichismo y religión en las sociedades primitivas*.

4. Godelier, "Infraestructura."

5. Jean Baudrillard, *Crítica de la economía política del signo*, p. 111.

6. The humorist Carlos del Peral imagined a similar conceit in his text "Viaje al país del turismo," published in the magazine *Crisis* in 1973. One knows that Disneyland and Disneyworld have put into practice imperfect approximations of these fantasies in real life.

5. From the Market to the Boutique: When Crafts Migrate

1. The reader will find a good account of the economic structure of these markets in the article by Luisa Paré, "Tianguis y economía capitalista," and in the previously cited work by Diskin and Cook on markets in Oaxaca. Those in Michoacán were studied at length by John W. Durston in his book *Organización social.* For fairs tied to religious events and their connection to regional market networks, see the study by Guillermo Bonfil, "Introducción al ciclo de ferias de Cuaresma en la región de Cuautla, Morelos (México)," pp. 167–202.

2. Bronislaw Malinowski and Julio de la Fuente, *La economía de un sistema de mercados en México,* p. 20.

3. J. Martín Barbero, "Prácticas de comunicación en la cultura popular," p. 244.

4. Bourdieu, *Distinction,* p. 35.

5. Alice Littlefield, "The Expansion of Capitalist Relations of Production in Mexican Crafts," pp. 471–488.

6. Novelo, *Artesanías,* p. 128.

7. Bourdieu, *Distinction,* pp. 257–258.

8. Cirese, *Ensayo,* pp. 25–41.

9. Baudrillard, *El sistema de los objetos,* p. 101.

10. Besides Victoria Novelo's book and the collection of studies from the *I Seminario sobre la problemática artesanal,* both cited above, see Andrés Medina and Noemí Quezada, *Panorama de las artesanías otomíes del Valle del Mezquital.*

11. The distinction between residual and emergent culture comes from Raymond Williams, *Marxism and Literature.*

6. *Fiesta* and History: To Celebrate, to Remember, to Sell

1. Giménez, *Cultura popular,* pp. 164–165.

2. The debate has been reviewed in Agnés Villadary, *Fête et Vie Quotidienne.*

3. *Noche de muertos,* brochure by the Office for Tourism of the Government of Michoacán, Morelia, n.d.

4. Pedro Carrasco, *El catolicismo,* p. 148.

5. Van Zantwijk, *Los servidores,* p. 148.

6. Giménez, *Cultura popular,* p. 161.

7. Cirese, *Ensayo,* chapter on "El ceremonial: celebraciones, operaciones, reproducciones."

8. Roberto de Matta, *Carnavais, malandros, heróis—para una sociologia do dilema brasileiro,* pp. 32, 33.

9. Michel Freitag, "De la ville-société a la ville millieu," pp. 25–27. Marianne Mesnil, *Trois essais sur la fête—du folklore a l'ethnosémiotique,* pp. 12–13.

Conclusion: Toward a Popular Culture in Small Letters

1. Two brave attempts in this direction are the article by Roberto Díaz Castillo, "Lo esencial en el concepto de arte popular," and the one by Mirko Lauer, "La mutación andina."

2. Juan Antonio Ramírez, *Medios de masas e historia del arte,* p. 265.

3. Cirese, *Ensayo*, p. 56.
4. Bertold Brecht, *Escritos sobre teatro*, p. 63.
5. Jorge Luis Borges, "Historia universal de la infamia," p. 295.
6. Cf. Dinerman, *Los tarascos*, cited above, particularly chap. 6, which offers well-documented and well-presented data on the nature of incompatibilities between Indian and capitalist social relations.

Bibliography

Aguirre Beltrán, Gonzalo. *El proceso de aculturación.* Mexico City: Universidad Nacional Autónoma de México (UNAM), 1957.

Althusser, Louis. *Ideología y aparatos ideológicos del Estado.* Mexico City: ENAH, 1975, p. 15.

———. "Ideología y aparatos ideológicos del Estado," in *La filosofía como arma de la revolución.* 9th ed. Cuadernos de Pasado y Presente, no. 4. Mexico City: Siglo XXI, 1979.

Arizpe, Lourdes. *Indígenas en la ciudad de México—el caso de las "Marías."* Mexico City: SepSetentas, 1979.

Atl, Doctor. *Las artes populares en México.* Mexico City: Editorial Cultura, 1921.

Bartra, Armando. *La explotación del trabajo campesino por el capital.* Mexico City: Editorial Macehual, 1979.

Bartra, Roger. *Estructura agraria y clases sociales.* Mexico City: Era, 1974.

Bataille, George. *La parte maldita.* Barcelona: Edhasa, 1974.

Bate, Luis F. *Sociedad, formación económico-social y cultura.* Mexico City: Ediciones de Cultura Popular, 1978.

Baudrillard, Jean. *Crítica de la economía política del signo.* Mexico City: Siglo XXI, 1974.

———. *El sistema de los objetos.* Mexico City: Siglo XXI, 1969.

———. *La société de consommation.* Paris: Gallimard, 1970.

Beals, Ralph L. *Cherán: A Sierra Tarascan Village.* Washington, D.C.: Smithsonian Institute, 1944.

Bonfil, Guillermo. "Introducción al ciclo de ferias de cuaresma en la región de Cuautla, Morelos (México)," *Anales de Antropología,* vol 7. Mexico City: 1971, pp. 167–202.

———. *Utopia y revolución: El pensamiento político contemporáneo de los indios en América Latina.* Mexico City: Nueva Imagen, 1981.

Borges, Jorge Luis. "Historia universal de la infamia," in *Obras completas.* Buenos Aires: Emecé, 1974, p. 295.

Bourdieu, Pierre. *L'amour de l'art—les musées européens et leur public.* Paris: Minuit, 1969.

———. *Distinction: A Social Critique of the Judgement of Taste.* Translated by Richard Nice. Cambridge, Mass.: Harvard University Press, 1984.

———. *The Logic of Practice.* Translated by Richard Nice. Stanford, Calif.:

Stanford University Press, 1990.

———. *Reproduction in Society, Education and Culture.* Translated by Richard Nice. London and Beverly Hills: Sage, 1977.

Brand, Donald, and José Correa Nuñez. *Quiroga, a Mexican Municipio.* Washington, D.C.: Government Printing Office, 1951.

Brecht, Bertold. *Escritos sobre teatro.* Buenos Aires: Nueva Visión, 1951; vol. 2, 1973.

Bronzini, Giovanni Battista. *Cultura popolare—dialettica e contestualitá.* Bari: Dedalo Libri, 1980.

Burra, Ventakapiah. "Adaptación de la sociedad tradicional a la moderna sociedad de masas," *Diógenes,* no. 33, 1961.

Carbonaro, Antonio, and Arnaldo Nesti. *La cultura negata—caratteri e potenzialitá della cultura popolare.* Rimini and Florence: Guaraldi Editore, 1975.

Carrasco, Pedro. *El catolicismo popular de los tarascos.* Mexico City: SepSetentas, 1976.

Caso, Alfonso. "El arte popular mexicano," *México en el arte,* no. 12, 30 November 1952.

———. "La protección de las artes populares," *América Indígena,* Instituto Indigenista Interamericano, Mexico City, 1942.

Castile, George Pierre. *Cherán: la adaptación de una comunidad tradicional de Michoacán.* Mexico City: Instituto Nacional Indigenista (INI), 1974.

Castrillón V., Alfonso. "¿Arte popular o artesanía?" Reprint from *Historia y Cultura,* no. 10, Lima, 1978.

Chacón, Alfredo. *Curiepe—ensayo sobre la realización del sentido en la actividad mágico-religiosa de un pueblo venezolano.* Caracas: Universidad Central de Venezuela, 1979.

Cirese, Alberto M. *Cultura egemonica e cultura subalterna.* Palermo: Palumbo Editore, 1976.

———. *Ensayo sobre las culturas subalternas.* Mexico City: Centro de Investigaciones Superiores del INAH, Cuadernos de la Casa Chata, no. 24, 1979.

———. *Intellettuali, folklore, instinto de classe.* Turin: Einaudi, 1975.

———. *Ogetti, segni, musei.* Turin: Einaudi, 1977.

Contreras, Ariel. "Economía pequeño mercantil y mercado capitalista," *Historia y Sociedad,* no. 12, 2d period.

Cox, Harvey. *The Feast of Fools.* Cambridge, Mass.: Harvard University Press, 1969.

De la Rea, Alonso. "Crónica de la Orden de N. Seráfico P. S. Francisco, provincia de San Pedro y San Pablo de Michoacán en la Nueva España (1643)." Mexico City, 1882.

Del Peral, Carlos. "Viaje al país del turismo," *Crisis,* no. 16, Buenos Aires, 1973.

De Matta, Roberto. *Carnavais, malandros, heróis—para una sociología do dilema brasileiro.* Rio de Janeiro: Zahar Editores, 1980.

Díaz Castillo, Roberto. *Folklore y artes populares.* Guatemala City: Editorial Universitaria, 1968.

———. "Lo esencial en el concepto de arte popular," *Cuadernos Universitarios,* Universidad de San Carlos de Guatemala, no. 7, March–April 1980.

Dinerman, Ina R. *Los tarascos, campesinos y artesanos de Michoacán,* Mexico City: SepSetentas, 1974.

Diskin, M., and S. Cook. *Mercados de Oaxaca.* Mexico City: INI, 1975.

Durston, John W. *Organización social de los mercados campesinos en el centro de Michoacán.* Mexico City: INI, 1976.

Duvignaud, Jean. *Fêtes et civilizations.* Geneva: Librairie Weber, 1973.

Eco, Umberto. *Apocalípticos e integrados ante la cultura de masas.* Barcelona: Lumen, 1968.

———. *Tratado de semiótica general.* Mexico City: Nueva Imagen, 1977.

Eliade, Mircea. *Lo sagrado y lo profano.* Madrid: Ediciones Guadarrama, 1967.

Erazo Fuentes, Antonio. "Sobre la preservación de valores de uso de carácter folklórico," *Centro de Estudios Folklóricos,* Universidad de San Carlos de Guatemala, 1976.

Espejel, Carlos. *Artesanía popular mexicana.* Barcelona: Editorial Blume, 1977.

———. *Cerámica popular mexicana.* Barcelona: Editorial Blume, 1975.

Establet, Roger. "Culture et idéologie," *Cahiers Marxistes Leninistes,* Paris, no. 12–13, July–October 1966.

Fernandes, Florestan. *Folklore e mudança social na cidade de São Paulo.* 2d ed. Petropolis: Voces, 1979.

Fernández Retamar, Roberto. *Calibán: apuntes sobre la cultura de nuestra América.* Buenos Aires: La Pléyade, 1973.

Fonart. *I Seminario sobre la problemática artesanal.* Mexico City: FONART-SEP, 1979.

Foster, George M. *Las culturas tradicionales y los cambios técnicos.* Mexico City: Fondo de Cultura Económica, 1964.

———. *Tzintzuntzan.* Mexico City: Fondo de Cultura Económica, 1972.

Freitag, Michel. "De la ville-societé a la ville millieu," *Sociologie et Societé,* Presses de l'Université de Montréal, vol. 3, no. 1, May 1971.

Galbraith, Bessie. "Artesanía," *Caminos del Aire,* Mexico City, Mexicana de Aviación, March–April 1980.

Gamio, Manuel. "El aspecto utilitario del folclore," *Mexican Folkways,* vol. 1, no. 1, June–July 1925.

———. *Forjando patria.* Mexico City: Porrúa, 1960.

———. "Posibilidades del arte indígena en México," *Boletín de la Unión Panamericana,* Washington, D.C., 1924.

García Canclini, Néstor. *Arte popular y sociedad en América Latina.* Mexico City: Grijalbo, Colección Teoría y Praxis, no. 38, 1977.

———. "Artesanías e identidad cultural," *Culturas,* Paris, UNESCO, vol. 6, No. 2, 1979.

———. *Culturas híbridas. Estrategias para entrar y salir de la modernidad.* Mexico City: Grijalbo-CNCA, 1990. (Translation from University of Minnesota Press, forthcoming.)

———. *La producción simbólica—teoría y método en sociología del arte.* Mexico City: Siglo XXI, 1979.

Giménez, Gilberto. *Cultura popular y religión en el Anahuac.* Mexico City: Centro de Estudios Ecuménicos, 1978.

Godelier, Maurice. *Economía, fetichismo y religión en las sociedades primitivas.* Mexico City and Madrid: Siglo XXI, 1978.

―――. "Infraestructura, sociedad e historia," *Cuicuilco*, Mexico City, 1980, no. 1.

Graburn, Nelson H. H. (ed.). *Ethnics and Tourist Arts*. Berkeley: University of California Press, 1976.

Gramsci, Antonio. *Los intelectuales y la organización de la cultura*. Mexico City: Juan Pablos Editor, 1976.

―――. *Literatura y vida nacional*. Mexico City: Juan Pablos Editor, 1976.

―――. *El materialismo histórico y la filosofía de Benedetto Croce*. Buenos Aires: Nueva Visión, 1973.

Guía turística de la Asociación Mexicana Automovilística. 10th ed. Mexico City: Asociación Mexicana Automovilística, 1980.

Guzmán, Alejandro. *Artesanos de la sierra norte de Puebla*. Mexico City: Dirección General de Arte Popular, 1977.

Hoggart, Richard. *The Uses of Literacy*. London: Chatto & Windus, 1957.

Instituto Nacional Indigenista (INI). *30 años después, revisión crítica*. Mexico City: INI, 1978.

Kroeber, A., and C. Kluckhohn. *Culture. A Critical Review of Concepts and Definitions*. Cambridge, Mass.: Peabody Museum, 1952.

Lauer, Mirko. "La mutación andina," *Sociedad y Política*, no. 8, Lima, February 1980.

Leclerc, Gérard. *Anthropologie et colonialisme*. Paris: Fayard, 1972.

Lefebvre, Henri. *De lo rural a lo urbano*. 4th ed. Barcelona: Península, 1978.

Leiris, Michel. "Folklore y cultura viva," in Robert Jaulin et al., *El etnocidio a través de las Américas*. Mexico City: Siglo XXI, 1976.

Lévi-Strauss, Claude. *Antropología estructural I*. Buenos Aires: Eudeba, 1968.

―――. *Antropología estructural II*. Mexico City: Siglo XXI, 1979.

―――. *Arte, lenguaje, etnología*. Mexico: Siglo XXI, 1968.

―――. *El pensamiento salvaje*. Mexico City: Fondo de Cultura Económica, 1964.

―――. *Race et histoire*. Paris: Editions Gouthier-UNESCO, 1961. (There is a Spanish translation in his *Antropología estructural*.)

Linton, Ralph. *Acculturation in Seven American Indian Tribes*. New York: D. Appleton-Century, 1941.

Lise Pietri, Anne. "La artesanía: un factor de integración del medio rural," in Iván Restrepo (ed.), *Conflicto entre ciudad y campo en América Latina*. Mexico City: Nueva Imagen, 1980.

Lise, Anne, and René Pietri. *Empleo y migración en la región de Pátzcuaro*. Mexico City: INI, 1976.

Lise, Pierre. *Las artesanías y pequeñas industrias en el estado de Michoacán*. Pátzcuaro: CREFAL, 1964.

Littlefield, Alice. "The Expansion of Capitalist Relations of Producton in Mexican Crafts," *Journal of Peasant Studies*, 1980, pp. 471–488.

Lombardi Satriani, L. M. *Antropología cultural—análisis de la cultura subalterna*. Buenos Aires: Galerna, 1975.

―――. *Apropiación y destrucción de la cultura de las clases subalternas*. Mexico City: Nueva Imagen, 1978.

Maduro, Otto. *Religión y conflicto social*. Mexico City: Centro de Estudios Ecuménicos–Centro de Reflexión Teológica, 1980.

Mair, Lucy. *Native Policies in Africa*. New York: Negro Universities Press, 1969. (Orig. pub. 1936.)

Malinowski, Bronislaw, and Julio de la Fuente. *La economía de un sistema de mercados en México*. Acta Antropológica, 2d period, vol. 1, no. 2. Mexico City: Escuela Nacional de Antropología e Historia, Sociedad de Alumnos, 1957.

Margulis, Mario. *Contradicciones en la estructura agraria y transferencia de valor*. Mexico City: El Colegio de México, 1979.

———. "La cultura popular," *Arte, sociedad, ideología*, Mexico City, 1977, no. 2.

Marín de Paalen, Isabel. *Historia general del arte mexicano. Etnoartesanías y Arte Popular*, vols. 1 and 2. Mexico City: Editorial Hermes, 1976.

Marroquín, Alejandro. *La ciudad mercado (Tlaxiaco)*. Mexico City: UNAM, 1957.

Martín Barbero, Jesús. "Prácticas de comunicación en la cultura popular," in Máximo Simpson Grinberg, ed., *Comunicación alternativa y cambio social*. Mexico City: UNAM, 1981.

Martínez Peñaloza, Porfirio. *Arte popular de México*. Mexico City: Panorama, 1981.

Medina, Andrés, and Noemí Quezada. *Panorama de las artesanías otomíes del Valle del Mezquital*. Mexico City: Instituto de Investigaciones Antropológicas, UNAM, 1975.

Mendieta y Nuñez, Lucio. *Los tarascos. Monografía histórica, etnográfica y económica*. Mexico City, 1940.

Mesnil, Marianne. *Trois essais sur la fête—du folklore a l'ethnosémiotique*. Brussels: Cahiers d'Étude de Sociologie Culturelle, 1974.

Moya Rubio, Víctor José. *Máscaras, la otra cara de México*. Mexico City: UNAM, 1978.

Nahmad, Sitton, et al. *7 ensayos sobre indigenismo*. Mexico City: INI, 1977.

Najenson, José Luis. *Cultura nacional y cultura subalterna*. Toluca: Universidad Autónoma del Estado de México, 1979.

Novelo, Victoria. *Artesanías y capitalismo en México*. Mexico City: SEP-INAH, 1976.

Novo, Salvador. "Nuestras artes populares," *Nuestro México* 1:5, Mexico City, July 1932, p. 56.

Olivera, Mercedes. "Estudio del proceso de desaparición-reproducción de la población indígena de México. Acercamiento teórico-metodológico." Manuscript presented to the symposium on Ethnic Studies of CISNAH, Cuernavaca, January 1979.

Paré, Luisa. "Tianguis y economía capitalista," *Nueva Antropología*, 1, no. 2, Mexico City, October 1975.

Paz, Octavio. *El laberinto de la soledad*. Mexico City: Fondo de Cultura Económica, 1964.

Pozas, Ricardo. "La alfarería de Patamban," *Anales del INAH*, vol. 3, sixth period, Mexico City, 1949, pp. 115–145.

Pozas, Ricardo, and Isabel H. de Pozas. *Los indios en las clases sociales de México*. 3d ed. Mexico City: Siglo XXI, 1973.

Propp, Vladimirja. *Edipo alla Luce del folclore*. Torino: Einaudi, 1975.

————. *Feste agrarie russe.* Bari: Dedalo Libri, 1978.

Quijano, Aníbal. *Dominación y cultura.* Lima: Mosca Azul, 1980.

Ramírez, Juan Antonio. *Medios de masa e historia del arte.* Madrid: Ediciones Cátedra, 1976.

Raza y clase en la sociedad postcolonial. Paris: UNESCO, 1978.

Redfield, Robert. *El mundo primitivo y sus transformaciones.* Mexico City: Fondo de Cultura Económica, 1966.

————. *Yucatán: una cultura en transición.* Mexico City: Fondo de Cultura Económica, 1944.

Rendón, Teresa. "Utilización de la mano de obra en la agricultura mexicana, 1940–1973," *Demografía y Economía* 10:3 Mexico City, 1976.

Ribeiro, Darcy. *Las Américas y la civilización.* 3 vols. Buenos Aires: Centro Editor para América Latina, 1969.

Rubín de la Borbolla, Daniel F. *Arte popular mexicano.* Mexico City: Fondo de Cultura Económica, 1974.

Rubín de la Borbolla, Daniel F., and Ralph L. Beals. "The Tarascan Project: A Cooperative Enterprise of the National Polytechnical Institute, Mexican Bureau of Indian Affairs and the University of California," *American Anthropology* 42, Menasha, 1940, pp. 708–712.

Schaeffer, Herwin. "The Craftsman in an Industrial Society," *British Journal of Aesthetics,* Autumn 1971.

Serbin, Andrés, and Omar González. *Indigenismo y autogestión.* Caracas: Monte Avila Editores, 1980.

Spicer, Edward. "Acculturation," in *International Encyclopedia of Social Sciences,* vol. 1. New York: Macmillan, 1968, pp. 21–27.

Stavenhagen, Rodolfo. *Problemas étnicos y campesinos.* Mexico City: INI, 1979.

Stromberg, Gobi. "El juego del coyote: platería y arte en Taxco," unpublished.

Thurot, J. M., et al. "Efectos del turismo en los valores socioculturales," *Estudios Turísticos,* no. 57–58, Madrid, January–June 1978.

Van Zantwijk, R. A. M. *Los servidores de los santos.* Mexico City: INI, 1974.

Villadary, Agnés. *Fête et vie quotidienne.* Paris: Les Editions Ouvrières, 1968.

Warman, Arturo. *La danza de moros y cristianos.* Mexico City: SepSetentas, 1972.

West, Robert C. *Cultural Geography of the Modern Tarascan Area.* Washington, D.C.: Smithsonian Institute, 1948.

Williams, Raymond. *Marxism and Literature.* Oxford: Oxford University Press, 1977.

Zaldívar Guerra, Maria. Luisa. *Consideraciones sobre el arte popular en México,* Sociedad Mexicana de Antropología, 13, Roundtable, Jalapa, September 1973.

Index

Aesthetics: concept of art, in Western, 107; of souvenirs, 81–83
Anthropology: views of, toward culture, 2–3, 4–7

Boutiques, vii, x, 76, 79, 80
Bracerismo, 91

Capitalist modernization, viii, ix, x, 8, 45, 47, 60, 64, 69, 82, 97, 103
Cargueros, 90, 91, 92, 97, 100, 101
Compadrazgo, 89, 116
Consumption: role of, in affecting production and circulation of crafts, 76–77
Crafts: as capitalist necessity, 45–47; character of, 28; commercialization of; disuse of, 74–75; globalization of, 7; uses of 77–79; as vantage point on culture, 69–71
Cultural apparatuses, 17, 19
Cultural capital, viii, 2, 16, 17, 18, 19, 21, 22, 37, 43
Cultural policies, x, 109, 110, 113
Cultural relativism, 5, 7, 8, 9, 15
Culture: defined, 10; peasant culture, 76, 84; popular culture, vii, viii, 1, 2, 21, 22, 23–25, 27–29, 38, 41, 43, 62, 69, 75, 84, 85, 100, 105–108, 111, 118; as social process of production, 11–13; subordi-
nate culture, 26; urban culture, 77, 82, 88

Day of the Dead, vii, 74, 98
Death, attitudes toward, 98–100
Declaration of the Rights of Man, 6
Democracy, conditions of, 67
Developmentalist technocratism, 109

Fairs, ix, x, 42, 43, 71, 74, 94, 97, 118n.1
Fiestas: characteristics of, 87–89; as dramatic oppositions, 87; as reflections of community life, 28–32; of Saints Peter and Paul, in Ocumicho, 90
FONART (National Fund for the Promotion of Arts and Crafts), 44, 49, 63, 65, 78, 95, 112, 117n.1

Globalization of culture, viii, 7, 8, 64

Huatzallari, 96

Ideology: as distinct from culture, 10; Marxist concept of, 10

Kitsch 107–108

Life-style: Bourdieu's definition of, 17; at risk, due to big industry, 111